Lillian Hellman
and August Wilson

MODERN
AMERICAN
LITERATURE
New Approaches

Yoshinobu Hakutani
General Editor

Vol. 37

PETER LANG
New York • Washington, D.C./Baltimore • Bern
Frankfurt am Main • Berlin • Brussels • Vienna • Oxford

Margaret Booker

Lillian Hellman and August Wilson

Dramatizing a New American Identity

PETER LANG
New York • Washington, D.C./Baltimore • Bern
Frankfurt am Main • Berlin • Brussels • Vienna • Oxford

Library of Congress Cataloging-in-Publication Data

Booker, Margaret.
Lillian Hellman and August Wilson:
dramatizing a new American identity / Margaret Booker.
p.   cm. — (Modern American literature; v. 37)
Includes bibliographical references and index.
1. Hellman, Lillian, 1906– —Knowledge—History. 2. American
drama—20th century—History and criticism. 3. Historical drama,
American—History and criticism. 4. National characteristics, American,
in literature. 5. Hellman, Lillian, 1906– —Views on race. 6. Wilson,
August—Knowledge—History. 7. African Americans in literature.
8. Group identity in literature. 9. Race in literature. I. Title.
II. Modern American literature (New York, N.Y.); v. 37.
PS3515.E343 Z58   812'.52—dc21   2002006580
ISBN 0-8204-6185-7
ISSN 1078-0521

Die Deutsche Bibliothek-CIP-Einheitsaufnahme

Booker, Margaret:
Lillian Hellman and August Wilson:
dramatizing a new American identity / Margaret Booker.
−New York; Washington, D.C./Baltimore; Bern;
Frankfurt am Main; Berlin; Brussels; Vienna; Oxford: Lang.
(Modern American literature; Vol. 37)
ISBN 0-8204-6185-7

Front cover illustration from August Wilson, *Fences,* directed by Margaret Booker,
Beijing People's Art Theatre, Beijing, China, 1996. Uncredited photo courtesy of the Beijing
People's Art Theatre. *From left to right:* Yan Yansheng (Bono), Margaret Booker (Director),
Cong Lin (Cory/Stage Manager), Gong Lijun (Rose), and Liang Guanhua (Troy).
Author photo by Chris Bennion

The paper in this book meets the guidelines for permanence and durability
of the Committee on Production Guidelines for Book Longevity
of the Council of Library Resources.

Peter Lang Publishing, Inc., 275 Seventh Avenue, 28th Floor, NY, NY 10001
www.peterlangusa.com

Printed in Germany

To my father, John Mackesy, whose response to "No Irish Hired Here" when he emigrated to America in 1929 resulted in great even-handedness and personal generosity in his treatment of others.

To my mother, Esther Martinique Mackesy, whose own desire for education and religious tolerance resulted in that of her three daughters.

For them both, I would wish a place in that heavenly kitchen where Lillian Hellman and August Wilson's mother cook up a storm!

Contents

Acknowledgments

I would like to thank the following:

Harry Elam for his gentle criticism, great humanity and generosity in picking up where Charles Lyons left off; Charles Lyons for his intellectual rigor, delicious sense of humor and belief in scholar/directors; Alice Rayner, William Eddelman and Michael Ramsaur for their careful reading and important suggestions; Peggy Cowles and the Ford Foundation for their financial support; August Wilson for his genius; Lloyd Richards for his love of new writing; Ingmar Bergman and Alf Sjöberg for their directorial acumen and inspiration; Walter Sokel for his urbane approach to literature; Karl Kramer for sharing his delight as resident scholar in rehearsal through our co-authorship of Chekhov translations; Bruce Thompson for his careful proofreading; the unflagging encouragement of friends and family; and last, but not least, Ron Davies, for his daily guidance and attention to detail which, when combined with his personal generosity, ultimately culminated in a finished manuscript.

Grateful acknowledgment is made to the following for permission to reproduce previously published material:

From *Four Black Revolutionary Plays* by Amiri Baraka. Copyright © by Amiri Baraka. Reprinted by permission of Sterling Lord Literistic, Inc.

From *The Collected Plays* by Lillian Hellman. Copyright © 1972 by Lillian Hellman. By permission of Little, Brown and Co. (Inc.).

From *Three: An Unfinished Woman, Pentimento, Scoundrel Time* by Lillian Hellman. Copyright © 1979 by Lillian Hellman By permission of Little, Brown and Co. (Inc.).

From *Ma Rainey's Black Bottom* by August Wilson, copyright © 1985 by August Wilson. Used by permission of Dutton Signet, a division of Penguin Putnam Inc.

Note on the Text

The works of Lillian Hellman and August Wilson cited in this book are from the following editions:

Hellman, Lillian. *The Collected Plays.* Boston & Toronto: Little, Brown & Co., 1972.

Hellman, Lillian. *Three: An Unfinished Woman, Pentimento, Scoundrel Time.* Boston & Toronto: Little, Brown & Co., 1979.

Wilson, August. *Ma Rainey's Blackbottom.* New York: Penguin (Plume), 1985.

Wilson, August. *Fences.* New York: Penguin (Plume), 1986.

Wilson, August. *Joe Turner's Come and Gone.* New York: Penguin (Plume), 1988.

Wilson, August. *The Piano Lesson.* New York: Penguin (Plume), 1988, 1990.

Wilson, August. *Two Trains Running.* New York: Penguin (Plume), 1992.

Wilson, August. *Seven Guitars.* New York: Penguin (Plume), 1996.

Lillian Hellman, *Toys in the Attic*, with John Gilbert (JULIAN), Eve Roberts (ANNA), and Megan Cole (CARRIE), directed by Margaret Booker, Intiman Theatre, Seattle, Washington, 1977. Photo by Chris Bennion.

August Wilson, *Fences*, with Liang Guanhua (TROY) and Gong Lijun (ROSE), directed by Margaret Booker, Beijing People's Art Theatre, Beijing, China, 1996. Uncredited photo provided by BPAT.

Diversity and the American Dream: Transformation from Within

> Postmodern culture with its decentered subject can be the space where ties are severed or it can provide the occasion for new and varied forms of bonding.... It's exciting to think, write, talk about, and create art that reflects passionate engagement with popular cultures, because this may very well be the central future location of resistance struggle, a meeting place where new and radical happenings can occur.
> —bell hooks, "Postmodern Blackness" (1993)

If we accept the theatre as an artistic arena for the "critical exchange" in which old constructs are dismembered and "a meeting place where new and radical happenings can occur," we can comparatively reexamine the works of Lillian Hellman and August Wilson—dramas which actively engage in the search for our national identity and the individual citizen's place in and responsibility towards it. Lillian Hellman and August Wilson are writers whose belief in freedom from oppression informs their work, yet their different gender and racial backgrounds necessarily produce different perspectives. Both are minority writers—writers of the gender (Hellman) and racial periphery (Wilson)—overturning the status quo. Theirs is a "resistance struggle" wherein Lillian Hellman moves female characters (black and white) center stage while August Wilson generates a twentieth-century chronicle of the African American odyssey.

Political activists in their youth, Lillian Hellman and August Wilson are moralists provoked by perceived human inequities exemplified in historical events (the Depression and the Civil Rights Movement). A revolutionary point of view—evidenced in Hellman's anti-fascism and resistance towards the House on Un-American Activities Committee and Wilson's involvement in the Black Power movement—informs their plays and their lives. Perhaps most remarkable of all, both are artistically and commercially successful playwrights whose work has found an audience in the cultural mainstream on Broadway and in theatres throughout the country. Their success points not only to the quality of their art, but also to their ability to take the pulse of the times. They express an evolving view of American identity, based in a contemporary interpretation of the American Constitution and the Bill of Rights, to a responsive, diverse public. Change (or the lack thereof) in the treatment of racial and gender difference signifies alteration in social roles and economic dependence/independence and thereby validates or challenges the state of American citizenship.

A belief in the American Dream characterizes national identity and simultaneously unites the plays of Hellman and Wilson. As Americans, who are we and what do we value? What is the nature of the "American Dream" to which we now subscribe, but in which we participate at different levels because of our socioeconomic and racial backgrounds?

Toni Morrison returns to the "well-fondled" notion of the American Dream and suggests that the escape from oppression in the Old World of Europe informed the emphasis on freedom and empowerment in the New World. While Toni Morrison's description of the American Dream is not unusual, her perception of the American notion of freedom simultaneously including slavery's practice of racial/socioeconomic oppression is. She sees "the presence of the unfree within the heart of the democratic experiment—the critical absence of democracy, its echo, shadow, and silent force in the political and intellectual activity of some not-Americans. The distinguishing features of the not-Americans were their slave status, their social status, and their color." Using examples from American literature, Morrison shows us how the white man's use of blackness becomes a means of self-definition in a frightening New World. Her exploration of boundaries as a means of defining a new American identity can be extrapolated to include not only racial/social difference but also a reciprocal situation wherein the outside defines the inside as much as the center defines the periphery. Morrison's analysis of the use of black characters to define the "new white man" can be applied to Lillian Hellman's portrayal of black women of great moral rectitude in her dramas and fictional biographies that delineate the "new white woman." Addie guides Zan to adulthood and independence in *The Little Foxes* and Coralee frees her mistress Lavinia Hubbard from the repression by Marcus to realize her dream to start a school for black children in *Another Part of the Forest*. Hellman's fictional biographies—*Three* (*An Unfinished Woman*, *Pentimento* and *Scoundrel Time*) and *Maybe*—abound with descriptions of nurse/nanny/housekeeper female role models, such as Helen or Caroline Ducky or Sophronia, whom Hellman credits with her moral development and sense of fairness.

> My own liking for black people maybe came a few days after I was born when I was put into the arms of a wet-nurse, Sophronia, an extraordinary woman who stayed on with us for years after. It was she who taught me to have feelings for the black poor, and when she was sure I did, she grew sharp and said it wasn't enough to cry about

black people, what about the miseries of poor whites. She was an angry woman and she gave me an anger, an uncomfortable, dangerous, and often useful gift.[1]

She also introduces a series of black men who range from Civil Rights activists like old George and Gene Carondelet, whom she meets while covering the 1963 March on Washington, to Martin Luther King and friends of Malcolm X. Her work includes junkies (Orin in *An Unfinished Woman*), black manservants (Cal in *The Little Foxes*, Jacob in *Another Part of the Forest*, Leon in *Autumn Garden*) who clarify the household pecking order of power and indicate any disruption, and Albertine's "fancy man" Henry, modeled on her Aunt Lily's real-life lover, who protects and guides both white mother and daughter in *Toys in the Attic*.

On the other hand, productive examination of inter-racial boundaries occurs when we reverse Morrison's project to explore the black man's use of whiteness in his own evolving quest for African American identity. August Wilson constructs a largely peripheral world of whiteness that throws the blackness of his central characters into relief. His evolving definition of the "new black man" seems to hear "a rustle of wind blowing across two continents"—Africa and America. His framing is largely an economic one containing white characters onstage and off who first buy and sell blacks, use them for free or cheap labor, commodify their music for profit, or incarcerate them if they don't play along with the system. With the exception of Selig in *Joe Turner's Come and Gone,* who points towards a future of connection and shared values, most white men mentioned in Wilson's plays are stereotypes even if specifically identified by name or historical period. In a world of black characters "wrestling" in a life and death struggle for their place in it, whiteness only serves to throw focus on Wilson's primary concern, the evolution of black identity with its roots in Africa and its dream in America.

Differences in point of view also serve to illuminate those elements that provide a basis for some ongoing notion of American identity held in common while simultaneously recognizing specific, distinguishing characteristics. United by the moral imperative of the American Dream—and their peripheral social positions—Lillian Hellman and August Wilson move formerly marginal characters to center stage. As advocates of a more humane and equitable world, they study American mores in specific historical contexts and examine the link between identity and responsibility—to oneself, one's community and to society as a whole.

Grappling with the positive and negative aspects defining contemporary, diverse American culture inevitably leads to a discussion of identity politics

---

[1]   Lillian Hellman, *Scoundrel Time,* 611–12.

informed by an understanding of national history. What is history? Who creates history? Whose history is it? What provides the basis of history? What is
the relationship between memory and history? Why does history exist? Why
does one create history? In *An Unfinished Woman*, Lillian Hellman declares:

> All through my childhood and youth I had an interest in all sharp turns of history.
> Once upon a time, I read a great deal about the French Revolution and the men who
> preceded it and predicted it, and if I found the English social changes more to my
> taste it was only because I am frightened of violence. I was completely at home,
> however, in the American Revolution, and, forgetting or not wanting to know all the
> economic reasons for it, I grew up in deep admiration for all men who said, "Enough
> is enough. We will stand no more."[2]

If we consider America as a nation of constantly changing refugees who seek
control over their own destiny, it is inevitable that a re-examination of our
story as a country and culture would occur. Each new group seeks
empowerment, replacing the Old World's limitations to freedom and possibility imposed by the barriers of class, race, and socioeconomic position. We
privilege a value system passed on by our "forefathers" in the Constitution
and the Bill of Rights. Yet the very concept of voting rights was originally
restricted in practice to white male property owners and a representative form
of government under which a slave, considered as property, was arithmeti-
cally rendered as 3/5ths of a man. Given the documented facts, it's no won-
der that feminist and African American scholarship views history as a
"master's narrative," which still contains a residue of oppression.

> The importance of history to me is simply to find out who you are and where you've
> been. It becomes doubly important if someone else has been writing your history. I
> think Blacks in America need to reexamine their time spent here to see the choices
> that were made as a people. I'm not certain the right choices have always been
> made. That's part of my interest in history—to say "Let's look at this again and see
> where we've come from and how we've gotten where we are now." I think if you
> know that it helps determine how to proceed with the future.[3]

For these two authors, the theatrical use of history is a means of combatting
oppression and promoting a new and evolving notion of citizenship. August
Wilson declares:

> So much of what makes this country rich in art and all manners of spiritual life is the
> contributions that we as African Americans have made. We cannot allow others to
> have authority over our cultural and spiritual products. We reject, without reserva-
> tion, any attempts by anyone to rewrite our history so as to deny us the rewards of

---

2   Lillian Hellman, *Unfinished Woman,* 204.
3   Kim Powers, "An Interview with August Wilson," *Theater* (Fall/Winter, 1984), 52.

our spiritual labors, and to become the cultural custodians of our art, our literature and our lives. To give expression to the spirit that has been shaped and fashioned by our history is of necessity to give voice and vent to the history itself.[4]

Their dramas situate the dilemmas of those once rendered "historyless" in an ongoing examination of human worth. What better place to give voice to the historyless, to bring the past into the present, than a theatre in which the performance dynamic is one of the present tense, a genre in which the past is made present? In stopping time for the length of a play, the authors "blast a specific era out of the homogeneous course of history" to elucidate the present. The dramas of Hellman and Wilson exist in that "state of emergency" which Walter Benjamin in *Illuminations* calls the rule rather than the exception for those who subscribe to the tradition of the oppressed.[5]

> To articulate the past historically...means to seize hold of a memory as it flashes up at a moment of danger. Historical materialism wishes to retain that image of the past which unexpectedly appears to man singled out by history at a moment of danger. The danger affects both the content of the tradition and its receivers. The same threat hangs over both: that of becoming a tool of the ruling classes.[6]

Thus, the play itself becomes one of Benjamin's "monads"[7] while the setting becomes a *lieu de mémoire*, to use Pierre Nora's term,

> where memory crystallizes and secretes itself at a particular historical moment, a turning point where consciousness of a break with the past is bound up with the sense that memory has been torn—but torn in such a way as to pose the problem of the embodiment of memory in certain sites where a sense of historical continuity persists.[8]

For a contemporary world involved in a quest to give recognition to gender and differing cultures, history in the sense of both documents and oral narratives becomes not just the context but the goal. Giving history to the historyless means expanding American history to include a citizenry of all races.

---

4 August Wilson, "The Ground On Which I Stand," *American Theatre* (New York, 9/96), 72.
5 Walter Benjamin, *Illuminations,* Hannah Arendt, ed. Harry Zohn, trans. (New York: Schocken Books, 1969), 263.
6 Benjamin, 255.
7 *Ibid.*
8 Pierre Nora, *Les Lieux de Mémoire* [English: *Realms of Memory: Rethinking the French Past,* Lawrence D. Kritzman, ed. Arthur Goldhammer, trans. (New York: Columbia UP, 1996)], v. 1, 284.

The ongoing perception of the enormous gulf between America's practices and promises prods both Hellman and Wilson to rewrite history. They both attempt to provide an antidote to the sense of disruption, rootlessness, and discontinuity of modern life by utilizing the processes of remembrance to move toward a greater understanding of our identity in the context of an evolving American tradition. Lillian Hellman once said: "We are a people who do not want to keep much of the past in our heads. It is considered unhealthy in America to remember mistakes, neurotic to think about them, psychotic to dwell on them." Cornel West's description of America as "a nation infamous for its brash will to historical forgetfulness" coincides with Hellman's, yet West goes on to point out that African Americans are the very ones who could not forget their own experience of slavery.[9] August Wilson agrees with West and urges African Americans to celebrate, rather than deny their history: "I'm taking each decade and looking at one of the most important questions that blacks confronted in that decade and writing a play about it," he says. "Put them all together and you have a history."[10]

As dramatists, Hellman and Wilson share a history both experienced directly in their own lives and heard about. Each undergoes a double diaspora, a migration from the old to the new world as well as one from the South to the North. Hellman's Jewish family migrated from Germany in the midnineteenth century to the deep South of Louisiana (New Orleans) and Alabama. She spent half the year in New Orleans and the other half in New York until she was sixteen years old. Her South was loved and lived in. She heard family stories of immigration, their role in the Civil War and Reconstruction, money made from the backs of Negroes, dying Southern aristocrats, and the vigor of the new and ruthless industrialists who moved northward where they lived off their southern profits in high style. Her relatively poor aunts (her father's sisters) exposed her to the restrictions of little money and the small generosities of shared life in a black and white community. She learned a sense of fair play from her black nanny Sophronia. In addition she developed a love for farming and bayou country, fishing and food, and a fascination for the South's steamy Gothic side evident in the use of drugs, the operations of the Mafia, and its interracial scandals. From there she moved to New York (the city and Hardscrabble Farm), worked in Hollywood, and finally settled on Martha's Vineyard. Her travels through Europe and Russia during the

---

9   Genevieve Fabre & Robert O'Meally, eds. *History and Memory in African-American Culture* (New York: Oxford UP, 1994), 3.

10   Hilary DeVries, "August Wilson—a new voice for black American theater," *The Christian Science Monitor* (10/16/84), 31.

Thirties and Forties gave her a global perspective and an outsider's look at American life and mores.

Like Hellman, Wilson claims a double diaspora, although different. Wilson cites the Middle Passage from Africa to America and the migration from the South to the North. However, his American South, the "ancestral homeland"[11] was not lived in by him, but created by him as a northern black man. Listening to tales in his home and on the street corner in Pittsburgh and inspired by both his black mother from North Carolina and the Black Power movement, Wilson assembled a collective history of southern stories revolving around slavery, reconstruction, and the northward migration, yet he claimed African culture as well. Both Wilson and Hellman reactivate the processes of remembrance to alert us to our American status quo and potential. To counteract the danger to his community's well-being, Wilson assumes the role of artist/shaman as the carrier of memories constructing a largely unrecognized history voiced by ordinary people protected by their neighborhood sanctuary.

The settings of both Hellman and Wilson plays serve a metaphorical function. They give us glimpses of cultures under attack. These settings house "moments of danger." Recognizing that there is "no document of civilization that is not at the same time a document of barbarism"[12]—whether it be the building of the Pyramids or the great cities of America—these two writers create a "real state of emergency." In their plays, memory attaches itself to sites and history to the event. The resulting matrix contains a dangerous conflict that liberates the constant quest for individual and social justice. This belief in the American Dream links August Wilson and Lillian Hellman, provides the basis for their artistic commitment, creates a bond with their popular audience, and promotes a new notion of citizenship.

---

11 August Wilson, "The Ground On Which I Stand," *American Theatre* (New York, 9/96), 72.
12 Benjamin, 256.

CHAPTER ONE

Political Activism and Moral Imperatives in the Theoretical Context

Within the time capsule of a mimetic and/or metaphorical representation of the world known and unknown, the theatre is the very site that exposes, shatters, and ultimately conjoins new perspectives on human identity, encompassing and validating otherness, before an audience which has chosen to be there. By its nature, the theatrical space provides the environment for a dialogue between performers of the text and an audience that decides to participate as evidenced by their voluntary attendance and purchase of tickets. The theatre is both a consentual and consensual environment which

> calls attention to those shared sensibilities which cross the boundaries of class, gender, race, etc., that could be fertile ground for the construction of empathy—ties that would promote recognition of common commitments, and serve as a base for solidarity and coalition.[1]

Inter- and intra-societal differences require some kind of information conduit for the communication of their specific value in an increasingly global, anonymous marketplace as well as a communication system that allows them all to function in some form of hopefully peaceful/productive coexistence.

Hellman and Wilson use the theatre to advocate human liberation. Both authors see language as a medium capable of coordinating action and the theatrical space as a place to service the ongoing human need for some sense of human agency in the face of an ever-expanding technological universe. Habermas, in his brilliant "Modernity: An Unfinished Project," describes

> [m]any different occasions for discontent and protest...wherever a one-sided process of modernization, guided by criteria of economic and administrative rationality, invades domains of life [or the "life world"] which are centred on the task of cultural transmission, social integration, socialization and education, domains orientated towards quite *different* criteria, namely towards those of communicative rationality.[2]

---

[1] bell hooks, "Postmodern Blackness," *A Postmodern Reader* (New York: State University of New York P, 1993), 518.

[2] Jürgen Habermas, "Modernity: An Unfinished Project," in *Habermas and the Unfinished Project of Modernity*, ed. Maurizio Passerin d'Entrèves and Seyla Benhabib (Cambridge: Polity Press, 1996), 44.

To solve the problems of late capitalism's colonization of the "life world" and its destruction of the traditional bases of communication contained therein, Habermas embeds rationality into language and advocates his "Theory of Communicative Action." By doing so, he does not eliminate the inclusion of postmodernist awareness of context and relational signification, but allows those validity-beliefs existing in the "life world" to become subject to a kind of disruptive evaluation through communicative reason. This disruptive gap between technological systems and the culture of the "life world," is summarized succinctly by Anthony Giddens as

> the taken-for-granted universe of daily social activity; saturation of communicative action by tradition and established ways of doing things; pre-interpreted set of forms of life, within which everyday conduct unfolds.[3]

The gap also results in the displacement of knowledge from the culture of a community into the hands of experts and creates a feeling of detachment and ennui in the society itself. Hence, the great need for a conduit like the theatre to bridge the gap, to explore the interstices, to allay a sense of helplessness in its all-too-human audience.

David Ingram in "The Subject of Justice" extends the theory of communicative action to a demand for political justice in capitalistic society.

> Since the dominance of money in capitalist democracies threatens the autonomy of the other spheres of justice and violates what Lyotard calls 'the justice of pluralities' and what Habermas, under the very different rubric of health, designates the 'integrity of a form of life,' its influence must at least be curtailed or confined more thoroughly to the sphere of commodity exchange than it presently is.[4]

It is precisely this disruptive evaluation presented by author and production to a consensual audience that provides the engine for the dramas of Wilson and Hellman. It is an engine fuelled by their own sense of responsibility as American citizens—a responsibility to act and a responsibility to otherness.[5] These two writers espouse a work ethic that demands equitable reward and a recognition that women and African American members of American society

---

3   Anthony Giddens, *Social Theory and Modern Sociology* (Stanford: Stanford UP, 1987), 232.

4   David Ingram, "The Subject of Justice," in *Habermas and the Unfinished Project of Modernity*, 29.

5   There is, however, a major shift in emphasis produced by differing ethical orientations between modernists and postmodernists. D'Entrèves contrasts Habermas and the postmodernists in their "two different senses of responsibility: a responsibility to *act* versus a responsibility to *otherness*" (2). I would like to suggest that the work of Hellman and Wilson incorporates both notions of responsibility.

are as valuable as any other of its citizens. Character, behavior, and mode of expression expose "otherness" and summon up solutions to exclusion from the promised American experience.

In the theatre, the viewing audience may or may not be familiar with or agree with the situation presented onstage, but the work of art itself becomes a physically shared experience in any case. The public exposure of "otherness" onstage can open a new "life world" to the audience and simultaneously revise racial and gender stereotypes as well as introduce an expanded view of American history beyond so-called "master narratives." Hellman pushes Regina Giddens directly into the commercial arena, usually reserved for men in 1900 America, and elevates her African American nanny, Addie (who is Zan's guardian), to the level of moral arbiter. August Wilson not only moves his black characters center stage, but takes us into urban ghettoes and draws his largely white audience into the African American experience itself.

To do this within the parameters of the theatre, Wilson introduces a form of language communication, Signifyin(g), integral to the black community whose mores and history find their expression in modes of provocative storytelling that reach back to African oral narratives and interpretive rituals tied to the religious beliefs and practices of the Yoruba in Nigeria and the Fon in Benin and transmitted orally through the diaspora of the Middle Passage. Henry Louis Gates, Jr., in his groundbreaking book *The Signifying Monkey*, examines the black vernacular in its "singular role as the black person's ultimate sign of difference, a blackness of the tongue. It is in the vernacular that, since slavery, the black person has encoded private yet communal cultural rituals."[6] His comparative examination of Esu-Elegbara, the Yoruban trickster and messenger of the gods, with his African American counterpart, the Signifying Monkey, exposes their shared function as interpreters who linguistically connect "truth with understanding, the sacred with the profane, text with interpretation" (6).

However, Gates believes that "free of the white person's gaze, black people created their own unique vernacular structures and relished in the double play that these forms bore to white forms. Repetition and revision are fundamental to black artistic forms" (xxiv). The difference between standard English signification ["denoting the meaning the term conveys or is intended to convey" (46)] within the Saussurian constellation of signification, signifier, and signified, and black English Signifyin(g), lies in its revision as a rhetorical function. Emphasis falls on the Signifier and foregrounds the style,

---

6   Henry Louis Gates, Jr., *The Signifying Monkey: A Theory Of Afro-American Literary Criticism* (New York & Oxford: Oxford UP, 1988), xix.

the way in which the story is told (45). Gates defines Signification as a black rhetorical strategy involving the obscuring of apparent meaning through "double-voiced utterance," a technique emanating directly from and executed in the Signifying Monkey tales associated with slavery (51–52). Black written texts assume the guise of oral narration.

Wilson employs the device of "loud talking," one of Gates' forms of Signification—

> speaking to a second person remarks in fact directed to a third person, at a level just audible to the third person. A sign of the success of this practice is an indignant "What?" from the third person, to which the speaker replies, "I wasn't talking to you." Of course, the speaker was, yet simultaneously was not. (82)[7]

So it is that Holloway can deliver his "Ain't no money in niggers working" speech to Memphis onstage and the mostly white audiences of August Wilson's *Two Trains Running* simultaneously. In *The Piano Lesson,* the black characters onstage and the audience in the house can hear Hambone, the black man standing up for his economic fair share, demand his ham from Lutz, who refuses to pay him properly for his fence repair. Seth and Bertha can comment on Bynam's "mumbo jumbo" nonsense seen in his ritual pigeon killing in *Joe Turner's Come And Gone* and indirectly prepare the audience for Herald Loomis's ritual bloodletting. Boy Willie can talk about, and eventually confront, Sutter's Ghost in *The Piano Lesson.*

Wilson's work, filled with the stories of "brothers exchanging tales,"[8] executes his overriding aim to project his hundred-year chronicle of the black experience onto the canvas of American history and simultaneously draw his predominantly white audience into acknowledging the actuality of that experience. Mark William Rocha rightly identifies the purpose behind Wilson's rhetorical technique:

> The basic trick of Wilson as loud-talker is to engineer his addressee, the theater audience, into a position before a group of blacks in which a charge can be brought that otherwise would be rejected as being deliberately confrontational.... (124)

It is a "technique of indirect argument or persuasion"[9] meant for an audience to hear in two different ways: a version of the original utterance as the embodiment of its speaker's point of view and the second speaker's evalua-

---

7   See also Mark William Rocha's "American History as 'Loud Talking' in *Two Trains Running,*" in Alan Nadel, *May All Your Fences Have Gates: Essays on the Drama of August Wilson* (Iowa City: U of Iowa P, 1994), 116–132.

8   H. Rap Brown, as quoted in Rocha, "American History," 119 and Gates, 74.

9   Roger D. Abrahams, *Deep Down In The Jungle: Negro Narrative Folklore From The Streets Of Philadelphia* (Chicago: Aldine Publishing, 1970), 51–52.

tion of that utterance from a different point of view. As he himself admits, Wilson is truly revising history.

> These stories mean something different to these people [in *Two Trains*]. They're not just passing the time or entertaining themselves, they're creating and preserving themselves. In the oral tradition, stories are the way history gets passed down, so they better be told right. By "right" I mean in a way that's memorable. Africans judge a storyteller by how long he can hold an audience.[10]

Wilson, through his characters, speaks to his audience, in both a welcoming and purposive manner. "Loud talking" to both the black community and his largely white audience, Wilson (like the Signifying Monkey) compels us to study the problem of American History. Wilson's "loud talking" characters are meant to be heard by audiences of all races.

The characters imagined by Hellman and Wilson exist in a challenged "life world" and deal with the economy and the state as institutionalized forms of purposive-rational action and the basis of system integration as articulated by Habermas. Money and power become the circulating media affecting every individual's situation. A national/global market economy results in the sublation of black cultural differences and the commodification of the black "life world" in its role as a "counterculture of modernity."[11] The antidote to the reduction of human society to informational databanks and efficient performativity, however playfully manipulated by their users, lies in the American democratic experiment, an ongoing cultural exploration of difference both divisive and exhilarating.

A common commitment to a value system promising equal rights and opportunity under law expressed in the Constitution and its amendments, the Bill of Rights, and the Declaration of Independence, underlies the differences of gender, race, and period found in the works of Lillian Hellman and August Wilson. Although they are legacies of Enlightenment thought espousing essentializing narratives regarding the freedom and progress of mankind, these documents, always subject to reinterpretation through the legal system, provide a description of those rights to which every American believes himself/herself entitled as a citizen. The rights of voting and property ownership plus the abolition of slavery may not have been specified for women and blacks when these documents were first written, but both came about as a result of social unrest and an expanded reading and application of the texts' meaning to encompass gender and race. These eighteenth-century documents serve simultaneously as both "sites of memory" because they delineate hu-

---

10 Interview with August Wilson, Rocha, "American History," 126–27.
11 Paul Gilroy, *The Black Atlantic* (Cambridge: Harvard UP, 1993).

man rights, once denied in the Old World, to which every citizen in the New World of America is entitled, as well as a description of a specific form of democratic government. Today we reinterpret and apply these documents drafted at the dangerous historical moment of our revolution against England as legal and moral guidelines for the operation of our late capitalistic American society, which now contains a citizenry inclusive of women and African Americans once excluded from democracy's rights and privileges. Hence, there is a kind of shared moral spine that exists not only between the two authors but also between them and the populace at large.

Allowing for both consensus and difference, the American Constitution and the Bill of Rights themselves present an ongoing dialectic between a republican and a federalist view of government rooted in an attempt to balance the rights of an individual with those of the society as a whole. As David Ingram points out

> To take an example from American constitutional law, the republican interest in insulating democracy from the inegalitarian influence of money, knowledge and power opposes the federalist interest in retaining a marketplace of ideas and lifestyles in which unequal capacities for participation inevitably develop. If the former interest cedes priority to democratic majorities, the latter's respect for minorities does not—at least, not without the protection of judicial review.[12]

The spirit of dualist democracy informs an ever-changing re-interpretation of the original principles of government in a constant attempt to re-define the balance of American society.[13]

In today's postmodernist discourse, notions of human agency and justice inevitably complicate and expand upon this American legacy. Examining the interface between identity and responsibility in the works of Hellman and Wilson illuminates both the connection of modernism to postmodernism and the synthesis of both movements in the work of August Wilson. World War II, the Holocaust, and the American witch hunts of McCarthy's Fifties all appear to affect Hellman's notion of the importance of an individual's role in changing history, so explicitly broached in both *Watch On The Rhine* in the "good" German Kurt's participation in the resistance movement and *The Searching Wind* in career diplomat Alex Hazen's indecisiveness regarding the Fascists, and in Hellman's own behavior before the House Un-American Activities Committee. Like finely executed timepieces, Hellman's dramas present a linear view of history in which every action has its consequences.

---

12 David Ingram, "The Subject of Justice," in Jürgen Habermas, "Modernity: An Unfinished Project," in *Habermas and the Unfinished Project of Modernity*, ed. Maurizio Passerin d'Entrèves and Seyla Benhabib (Cambridge: Polity Press, 1996), 294–95.

13 *Ibid.*

Her later plays, *The Autumn Garden* and *Toys In The Attic*, which focus on the results of inactivity and wary self-interest, question the idea of human progression. The use and abuse of money and power, particularly in regard to women, permeates her dramas as well as her autobiographical fictions—*Pentimento*, *Unfinished Woman*, and *Scoundrel Time*. These three examine the reality of one's own experience and *Maybe* presents the possibility that there is no kind of objective reality at all.

August Wilson, on the other hand, did not experience World War II as an adult, but grew up in the postwar era when African Americans who had served in the military during World War II still did not vote and remained largely segregated. Postwar economic prosperity didn't reach far into the ghetto. The social upheaval he experienced was that of the Civil Rights and Black Power movements. His crisis was that of the race riots of the Sixties. Imbued with the activist values of the Black Power movement, Amiri Baraka's notion of the artist as a shaman for his people, Maulana Karenga's advocacy of a collective black economy providing shared sustenance for the community, Wilson, like Hellman, seeks to establish individual worth and economic parity within the American system. At the same time, he sets out to define the positive uniqueness of African American "otherness" before advocating a plan of action to achieve equal status. His work, chronicling the issues facing black Americans over 100 years, employs every tool, modernist or postmodernist, at his disposal. His seemingly realistic neighborhoods deal with the insignificant characters and events of a specific epoch, as Lukács describes in *The Historical Novel*, but Wilson's characters' circular, anecdotal revisions of history (all of the plays), musical and metaphorical style of narration (particularly in *Ma Rainey's Black Bottom* and *Seven Guitars*), and staged spiritual visions of the irrational or invisible (*Fences, The Piano Lesson* and *Joe Turner's Come And Gone*), describe a postmodernist approach to the world—a kind of serial and cumulative Lyotardian set of paralogisms. It is, however, a world in which human agency, "self-determination," is paramount and a sense of community, essential. The drama, for both authors, becomes both a cultural reminder and a means of cultural recovery. Theirs is, indeed, an ideological aesthetic.

The dramas of Lillian Hellman and August Wilson reflect the intellectual milieu and social context of two different periods in the twentieth century. Written primarily in the Thirties and Forties, Hellman's plays interact within the environment of the Depression years: the American intelligentsia's support of Marxism seen in the emergence of labor unions in America, of proletarian worker revolts in Europe and of the Soviet Union; and criticism of the rise of Fascism in Germany and Italy between and during the two world wars. August Wilson's dramas, written primarily during the Eighties and Nineties, reflect the values and greater expectations of the Civil Rights movement as well as his youthful participation in the Black Power movement of the Sixties. Wilson contextualizes his human dramas with current social issues. These include the shattering of the nuclear African American family from slavery onward; the northward migration of blacks from the South and the difficult adaptation of farm folk to city industry; the Depression; the odyssey of black professional athletes, musicians, laborers, and business/home owners into the respectable American work force; the re-entry of black veterans from World War II and Korea into the life of the old neighborhoods; and the demolition of African American communities within those same cities. His projected chronicle of ten plays purports to study the African American emergence from slavery to the present day and project it onto the larger American canvas of history and society.

Their respective early involvements in the political ferment of the Thirties and the Sixties shape the value systems under which Hellman and Wilson create their plays. In the Twenties and Thirties, many American writers, opposed to the socioeconomic ills of capitalist society, became admirers of Marx and Engels and joined a myriad of Communist front organizations; Lillian Hellman was no exception. In 1929 in New York, Hellman joined a John Reed Club under the control of Earl Browder and the Communist Party and campaigned for the passage of the Wagner Act allowing employees to bargain collectively and prohibiting employer discrimination against union members.[14] In 1935 she joined, along with Ruth Goetz, the League of Women Shoppers in New York and helped organize female laundry/house workers earning starvation wages. She even tried to start a union at Metro-Goldwyn-Mayer. Hellman, serving on the Board of Directors, played a major part in the union organization of the Screen Writers Guild.[15]

In Hollywood she participated in the Anti-Nazi League and the Western Writers Congress.[16] According to Joan Mellen, however,

> It was the very moment when under orders from the Comintern, the Party was discarding the revolutionary ideology, abandoning the ideals of Communism and socialism and the class struggle, and instead proclaiming its Americanism, its patriotism, its New Dealism and its antifascism. (102–103)

---

[14] Joan Mellen, *Hellman and Hammett* (New York: Harper Collins, 1996), 113.
[15] *Ibid.*, 128. See also Timothy J. Wiles, "Lillian Hellman's American Political Theater: The Thirties and Beyond," *Critical Essays on Lillian Hellman*, ed. Mark Estrin (Boston: G.K. Hall, 1989), 91–92.
[16] Mellen, 123.

As a "Roosevelt Bohemian," this stance suited Hellman perfectly. As an anti-fascist journalist, she reported on the Spanish Civil War and financially supported Hemingway's film about the anti-Franco Loyalists, *The Spanish Earth* (1937). She later wrote the semi-documentary film *North Star* in support of the Soviet Union despite the anti-Trotsky purges. Attacked for her refusal to give a benefit performance of *The Little Foxes* to support Finnish refugees because of their affiliation with Hitler, Hellman in *Pentimento* declared:

> nobody has ever been able to control me when I feel that I have been treated un-justly. I am, in fact, bewildered by all injustice, at first certain that it cannot be, then shocked into rigidity, then obsessed, and finally as certain as a Grand Inquisitor that God wishes me to move ahead, correct and holy. (486)

Undaunted, Hellman went on to pit European fascism against American isolationism in *Watch on the Rhine* in 1941.

Like many other writers of the 1930s, Hellman looked at the Great Depression as evidence of capitalism gone amok and depicted a Darwinian world of "haves" and "have nots" in her plays.[17] The class struggle of *The Little Foxes* and *Another Part of the Forest* simultaneously looked back at the ruthless greed of post-bellum industrialism and exposed the necessity of female charm and sexuality as the accepted mode of survival in lieu of economic dependence or power. Significantly Hellman did not write for the left-leaning Group Theatre, but chose the commercial Broadway stage where money, power and prestige had clout and fascination both onstage and off. Her campaign for equal pay for equal work found its expression on Broadway in the strike play *Days to Come* (1936), which just preceded *The Little Foxes*. This drama found like company with *Stevedore, Black Pit, Marching Song,* and *Waiting for Lefty*. The Women's Movement in the Sixties later lionized Hellman for her perception that "women's liberation is a matter of economics." As she told Bill Moyers in 1974: "it all comes down to whether you can support yourself as well as a man can support himself and whether there's enough money to make certain decisions for yourself rather than dependence."[18]

Hellman's assault on perceived injustice marked her entire life as well as her art. Perhaps her letter to HUAC is her most celebrated step.

---

[17] Wiles, 90.

[18] Bill Moyers, "Lillian Hellman: The Great Playwright Reflects on a Long, Rich Life," in *Conversations with Lillian Hellman*, ed. Jackson R. Bryer (Jackson, MS: UP of Mississippi, 1986).

Dear Mr. Wood,

As you know, I am under subpoena to appear before your committee on 21 May 1952.

I am most willing to answer all questions about myself. I have nothing to hide from your committee and there is nothing in my life of which I am ashamed. But I am advised by counsel that if I answer the committee's questions about myself, I must also answer questions about other people, and that if I refuse to do so, I can be cited for contempt.

To hurt innocent people whom I knew many years ago in order to save myself is, to me, inhuman and indecent and dishonorable. I cannot and I will not cut my conscience to fit this year's fashions, even though I long ago came to the conclusion that I was not a political person and could have no comfortable place in any political group.

I was raised in an old-fashioned American tradition and there were certain homely things that were taught to me: to try to tell the truth, not bear false witness, not to harm my neighbor, to be loyal to my country, and so on. It is my belief that you will agree with these simple rules of human decency and will not expect me to violate the good American tradition from which they spring. I would, therefore, like to come before your committee and speak only of myself.

Sincerely yours,

Lillian Hellman[19]

Jules Feiffer, in his graveside eulogy, commented on her concern with the government's assault on civil liberties during the last dozen years of her life and her subsequent formation of the Committee for Public Justice. "She chaired the meetings, helped raise agendas, and set up across the country a series of well-covered public meetings which described in detail the calculated erosion by the FBI, the CIA and the Justice Department on the First Amendment and our other constitutional rights."[20] Perhaps her old friend, novelist and fishing partner John Hersey said it best:

Anger was her essence.... It electrified a mood of protest.... It was a rage of the mind against all kinds of injustice.... In everything she wrote, and in her daily life, she fought against slander, greed, hypocrisy, cruelty and everything shabby and second-rate and dangerous in those in power....[21]

August Wilson shares this rage against social injustice. He too chooses the entertainment mecca of Broadway as the forum for his ideas voiced through his unique theatre of protest. Wilson acknowledges the influence of the Black Power movement following upon the Civil Rights movement of the

---

19 Text of HUAC Letter as quoted by Peter Adam, "Unfinished Woman," *Conversations*, 226.

20 Peter Feibleman, *Lilly: Reminiscences of Lillian Hellman* (New York: Avon Books, 1988), 355.

21 *Ibid.*, 361–62.

Sixties. He specifically cites Malcolm X, Amiri Baraka's *Four Revolutionary Plays,* and Maulana Karenga's "Seven Principles of Kwanzaa" as early influences on his thinking.[22]

In 1965, Wilson heard Malcolm's "Message to the Grass Roots." Wilson says, "it changed my life."[23] Wilson was to incorporate many of the concerns voiced in this early Malcolm speech about the black man's identity and his place in America into his plays. Malcolm X declared that the white hegemony didn't want black men, ex-slaves, here in America. He identified conflict within the black community and traced it to slavery's hierarchical ranking between house Negroes and field Negroes. Former slaves who had held privileged positions in the households of their owners loved the white man, while those who worked in the fields and survived as "gut-eaters" hated their masters. House Negroes were "Uncle Toms" whose Christian religion taught blacks to suffer peacefully, whereas the majority field Negroes retained their African religious and agrarian roots. Malcolm believed that this love/hate relationship with the white man was the source of divisiveness within the African American community. Only the acceptance of their shared history as ex-slaves would lead blacks towards an intelligent plan for a better future. Black people had to forget their differences, unite, and view the white man as the common enemy.

Malcolm believed the solution to this internal conflict lay in black nationalism. Citing examples from history—the French Revolution and the American Revolution as well as the European colonization of Africa which created slavery—Malcolm X declared:

> Look at the American Revolution in 1776. That revolution was for what? For land. Why did they want land? Independence. How was it carried out? Bloodshed.[24]

For Malcolm X, violence in Birmingham was real black revolution because it necessitated bloodshed and forced President Kennedy to send in the troops and Congress to enact the Civil Rights Bill. Unfortunately, in Malcolm X's view, whites had sabotaged the Civil Rights movement by co-opting "Negroes of national stature" like King, Evers, Randolph, Wilkins, Young and Powell to control their own people and by using them to invite labor (Walter Reuther), the Catholics, the Jews and liberal Protestants—"the same clique that put Kennedy in power"—to join the march on Washington. According to

---

22   Interview with Margaret Booker (Stanford, CA: Stanford University, 10/28/97); Mark William Rocha, "August Wilson and the Four B's: Influences," *August Wilson: A Casebook,* ed. Marilyn Elkins (New York & London: Garland Publishing Co., 1994), 3–16.
23   Booker interview.
24   Malcolm X, *Malcolm X Speaks* (New York: Grove Press, 1965), 7.

Malcolm X, the white power structure had employed "house negroes" to control the "field negroes" again (14–17).

Under Malcolm's influence, Wilson began an organization called the Afro-American Institute and acted as its "Defense Minister." In 1968, he and Rob Penny co-founded The Black Horizon Theatre in Pittsburgh "to raise the consciousness of the community."[25] He also joined the Centre Avenue Poets Theatre Workshop and Half Way Arts Gallery, where Pittsburgh's black artists and intellectuals discussed the writings of Ed Bullins, Richard Wesley, Ron Milner, Ishmael Reed, Maulana Karenga, Amiri Baraka and Malcolm X.[26] He wrote a play for director friend Claude Purdy who started the black Penumbra Theatre in St. Paul, and subsequently Wilson moved to Minneapolis.

Wilson's writing reflects Malcolm's ideas. He depicts the destructive results of blacks turning against each other in *Ma Rainey's Black Bottom* when Levee murders Toledo, when Troy nearly bludgeons his son to death in *Fences,* when King Hedley murders Floyd Barton. The need for recognition of slavery and an ancestral history finds its place in *The Piano Lesson* and *Joe Turner's Come and Gone.* Wilson sees the value of African religion in Herald Loomis's epiphany and in Berniece's "calling out" which, when combined with Boy Willie's confrontation, succeeds in routing Sutter's ghost when Avery's Christian exorcism fails.

Wilson agrees with Malcolm when he writes about "characters seeking to empower themselves through the process of becoming American. We have guideposts about how to do that, going all the way back to the Mayflower. American history shows the path."[27] Wilson recognizes the relationship of economic independence to self-respect and happiness. Wilson knows the governmental system and human rights described in the Constitution and the Bill of Rights including such things as property ownership, voting privileges, equal opportunity, and the right to bear arms:

> See now…if he [Boy Willie's grandfather] had his own land he wouldn't have felt that way. If he had something under his feet that belonged to him he could stand up taller. That's what I'm talking about. Hell, the land is there for everybody. All you got to do is figure out how to get you a piece. Ain't no mystery to life. You just got to go out and meet it square on. If you got a piece of land you'll find everything else fall right into place. You can stand right up next to the white man and talk about the

---

25   Booker interview.
26   Samuel G. Freedman, "A Voice From the Streets," *The New York Times*, 3/15/87, Section 6, 36.
27   Booker interview.

price of cotton...the weather, and anything else you want to talk about. If you teach
that girl that she living at the bottom of life, she's gonna grow up and hate you.[28]

The importance of land ownership to establish one's independence and identity as a free man is the basis of Boy Willie's desire to sell the family piano, a
piece of stolen property representing the family history and the bloody legacy
of slavery, to buy the Mississippi land his family had tilled as slaves. *Two
Trains Running* introduces a black business owner, Memphis, who learns to
use a white lawyer to get the city of Pittsburgh to pay him fair market value
for his soon-to-be-demolished diner property. He rejects a low offer from the
undertaker West, an example of blacks attempting to cheat blacks, and re-
ceives even more money from the city than he thought the property was
worth. Above all, Memphis plans to return to Jackson to reclaim the land he
legally owns from Stovall. Memphis earlier says that "Niggers killed
Malcolm," but he's returning to the South to "pick up the ball."[29] Wilson's
black nationalism now includes a return to the American South (not to Africa) as the new ancestral homeland as well as a pragmatic sense of the capitalistic system.

August Wilson, like fellow poet/dramatist Amiri Baraka, looked to
Maulana Karenga as an important theorist of black nationalism. Karenga was

> co-convenor and co-planner of all three National Black Power Conferences from
> 1966–68. He developed programs for and trained Black and Brown community or-
> ganizers and activists at the Social Action Training Center in Watts and the Center
> for Social Action at USC, and was a founding board member of the Brotherhood
> Crusade, the Black Congress and Mafundi Institute, all key organizations in Black
> development and struggle during the Sixties.[30]

The movement to turn to Africa as a source of roots and revitalization
was part of the thrust to define black identity in the Sixties. One of the organizations that sought "the rescue and reconstruction of our history, the redefinition of ourselves and our culture and a restructuring of the goals and
purpose of our struggle" was Karenga's US, a "Black nationalist organization
dedicated to the creation, recreation and circulation of culture."[31] US believed that the development of an ideology (Kawaida) containing a coherent
value system was crucial to the development and support of the Black struggle to evolve a new view of itself and eliminate the white (oppressor's) control over black mental attitudes. Kawaida promoted a kind of cultural

---

[28] August Wilson, *The Piano Lesson,* 91–92.
[29] August Wilson, *Two Trains Running,* 109.
[30] Maulana Karenga, *Kwanzaa* (Inglewood, CA: Kawaida Publications, 1977), 1.
[31] Karenga, 18.

revolution synthesizing tradition plus rational adaptation and development to define the place of the black community in America and in the world at large.

In 1966, Dr. Karenga created the African American holiday of Kwanzaa to promote the cultural unity of all with African background, continental or diasporan. Like all holidays, Kwanzaa is both a self-conscious cultural creation of a people aware and proud of its history and committed to its future as well as a political expression by those who recognize the power that comes from unity and self-determination (19). The ceremony utilizes traditions of agricultural African peoples that include gathering and celebration of past and present achievements, recognizes the legacy of the ancestors and provides models of creativity for emulation.

Despite the fact that most American Blacks are urban and not rural dwellers as in Africa, Karenga converts the celebratory nature of Kwanzaa's African harvest festival into a ritual of gathering, sharing, gift giving, and recognition of achievement. He claims a cultural heritage that goes back to the great civilizations of Egypt, Africa, and Islam and simultaneously continues the African oral tradition of elders passing on wisdom in the stories and toasts of the older American generation. These same people give acclaim and support to children, the centerpiece of Kwanzaa, in the context of a newly valued African American community. Above all, he praises the creativity which propels the community forward in the "continuing struggle" to make the world a better place for the next generation. It is not difficult to understand the significance of Karenga to two groundbreaking Black poet/dramatists, Amiri Baraka and August Wilson.

Central to Kwanzaa is a Black value system contained in the Nguzo Saba with its seven basic principles of Umoja (Unity in the family, community, nation and race), Kujichagulia (Self-determination), Ujima (Collective Work and Responsibility), Ujamaa (Cooperative Economics in the building and maintenance of businesses to profit the community), Nia (Restoration of the people to their "traditional greatness"), Kuumba (Creativity), and Imani (Faith in the African American people, including parents, children, teachers and leaders, and in the "righteousness and victory of our struggle.")[32] These seven guideposts establishing identity, personal worth and purpose serve as a support system for African Americans shattered by the breakup of family/community and the commodification of slavery and set adrift after abolition in America's capitalistic sea without the oars of education and practice of independence. A value system upholding the importance of unity within the Black community prevents implosion and provides a support network for people assuming new jobs and responsibility.

---

[32] Karenga, 9.

However, the thrust of owning one's own business upends the legacy of depending on the white man to provide work and discards the old notion of the black slave as property. While advocating the importance of work for pride in self and for acquisition of the means to advance in American society certainly sounds like the Puritan ethic, Karenga goes beyond the practice of "each man for himself" by advocating cooperative economics wherein African Americans share their profits, which in turn builds the community.

In addition to Malcolm X and Karenga, August Wilson points to the poetic style and black power principles of Amiri Baraka's *Four Revolutionary Plays* as another major influence on his writing.[33] Baraka links himself to the Kwanzaa ceremony and acts as the shaman artist when he employs the same Swahili opening greeting "Habari gani?" (What news?) in his introduction to *Four Black Revolutionary Plays:*[34]

> ...get in touch with Karenga and Tierinja
> "Hey Now, Hey now, Habari Gani"
> get in touch with the change, right now, athlete
> the status change from white to black
> we are winners and we will win from these devils all this land[35]

A role model for Wilson, Baraka proclaims his cultural antecedents in Africa and Egypt and his creative role as an artist thoroughly engaged in "the continuing struggle through which we will inevitably rescue and reconstruct our history and humanity in our own image and according to our own needs."[36] Here the artist becomes the conduit for the visceral energy of Black rage, seen in Wilson's ex-con "warrior spirits" like Troy or Booster, and channels it into a variety of black businesses.

> i am prophesying the death of white people in this land
> i am prophesying the triumph of black life in this land, and over all the world
> we are building publishing houses, and newspapers, and armies, and factories
> we will change the world before your eyes....[37]

In *Dutchman*, Baraka sees that without music and poetry, black men possessing only western rationalism would have to murder whites to be sane. The role of the artist, then, is extremely important in expressing anger to-

---

33   Booker interview.
34   Karenga, 98.
35   Amiri Baraka (LeRoi Jones), *Four Black Revolutionary Plays* (Indianapolis and New York: The Bobbs-Merrill Company, 1969), vii–viii.
36   Karenga, 95.
37   Baraka, vii–viii.

wards the *status quo*, but even more powerful in redirecting African American vitality and talent towards the development of a new "raiment of self" and sense of purpose in the ongoing, self-determined quest for freedom and a new sense of identity. Wilson was to take seriously this notion of the responsibility of the artist to his community.

Written in 1965—the year Wilson describes as that of his coming into manhood—*Experimental Death Unit #1* takes us to the streets where the author describes a sexual encounter between two white men on heroin and a black whore that culminates in the beheading of the two men by black soldiers. White Duff's remark that "I'm sacred as anyone, and I say the world is to the man who will take it" reverberates ironically in his own murder.[38] Wilson enables Sterling to take Hambone's long overdue ham.

A Black Mass (1965) particularly fascinates August Wilson because of its mythology.[39] For him, *A Black Mass* is an incomplete creation myth wherein black culture invents its own identity by celebrating the "beauties of creation; the beauties and strength of our blackness, of our black arts." Three black magicians dressed in robes with skullcap, fez, and African fila, accompanied by the Sun-ra music of eternal concentration and wisdom, and surrounded by signs in Arabic and Swahili, signify that "black is beautiful" in its history and in its diaspora. Unfortunately, Jacoub creates a vomiting "monster of whiteness" that co-opts the black woman, attacks its creator and ultimately the audience. Baraka warns the black man not to accommodate whiteness, for those who do will be appropriated like the black woman Tilla or murdered. At the end, the narrator urges killing whites instead. "Let us find them and slay them."[40] Wilson attacks black commodification of his music to white tastes in *Ma Rainey's Black Bottom* and in *Seven Guitars*, but does not advocate killing the white man.

Written in 1966, *Great Goodness of Life (A Coon Show)* presents the case of Court Royal, a post office worker who's accused of harboring a murderer, a young black man. A house negro, Court Royal defends himself thus:

> I'm a good man. I have a car. A home. A club. Please there's some mistake. Isn't there? I've done nothing wrong. I have a family. I work in the Post Office. I'm a supervisor. I've worked for thirty-five years. I've done nothing wrong. (56)

Terrorizing the black man with the rattling chains of slavery, the white man keeps Court Royal in his subservient place and prevents him from standing up for himself. Wilson follows Baraka in criticizing the ineffectuality of

---

[38]   Baraka, 5.
[39]   Booker interview.
[40]   Baraka, 39.

Avery, whose accommodation to the white man results in his inability to exorcise Sutter's ghost. Wilson, like Boy Willie, believes the black man can get his own turkey. When confronted with images of Malcolm, Patrice Lumumba, Rev. King, Marcus Garvey, and dead black children killed by the police, Court Royal, like Judas, denies he knows them. Instead the old man in a final rite ceremoniously kills his own shadow, his son. His soul becomes as "white as snow," and he goes off to bowl. Baraka shows us how the ex-slave's fear leads to the betrayal of his own offspring. So, in a metaphorical sense, the father's accommodation to the demands of whiteness leads him to the murder of his own son and the annihilation of freedom for the generation to come. Wilson advocates educating the young, like Maretha in *The Piano Lesson*, to know and celebrate their African American legacy so they can have better lives than their parents and a stronger sense of identity.

The split in the family becomes a metaphor for the conflict within the black community in *Madheart (A Morality Play)*, as it does in many Wilson plays—*Fences, Joe Turner's Come and Gone, The Piano Lesson,* and *Jitney*. Aspiring to be white sexual objects, a black mother sporting a red wig pimps for her blonde-wigged daughter. Both grovel before the white Devil Lady (whose "pussy" has been pasted over with a picture of Christ) conjured by the Black Man, yet another of Baraka's magician/artists. The two women become stereotypical whores condemned and relegated to those positions by white Christianity's "spirit of deadness" (71). The Black Man sees "My mother...and sister...crazy white things slobbering...God help me" (86) and watches them attack each other. When the natural Afro-haired Black Woman arrives, declares that black is beautiful, and appeals to the Black Man for love, his first reaction is to strike her. Baraka shows us that the assimilation of white qualities by Blacks causes conflict and death within the black community itself. He points out the need for Blacks to recognize their own beauty and self-worth and not to devalue each other as commodities in the way the white newspapers have portrayed them (81). Both authors advocate the development of a unified black community to support greater self-determination for African Americans.

Amiri Baraka in a sense is one of Wilson's "elders." An artist with a mission, he exemplifies the creative power so necessary to the development of a new African American identity. Baraka's use of visceral poetry, blues music, and ritual drama provided a serious model for the young August Wilson, a self-educated high school dropout at the age of fifteen. Wilson told Samuel G. Freedman of the *New York Times*:

> I think it was Amiri Baraka who said that when you look in the mirror you should see your God. All over the world, nobody has a God who doesn't resemble them.

> Except Black Americans. They can't even see they're worshipping someone else's God, because they want so badly to assimilate, to get the fruits of society. The message of America is "Leave your Africanness outside the door." My message is "Claim what is yours."[41]

Wilson also speaks of the need for revolution and advocates the use of violence against the oppressor through action or metaphor. In *Two Trains Running*, ex-con Sterling steals the long-owed ham to put in Hambone's coffin. In *Joe Turner's Come and Gone*, Loomis sheds his own past and metaphorically takes responsibility for his own future. Boy Willie attacks the ghost of Sutter, the slaveowner who had bought and sold his family, while Berniece plays the piano and calls upon their ancestors to assist. The theatre becomes a means of expressing and directing change.

After the examining the influences claimed by August Wilson—Malcolm X, Baraka, and Karenga—one sees the revolutionary purpose driving his plays. However, Wilson is above all an artist, a role he makes clear in his highly controversial speech "The Ground On Which I Stand," presented as the keynote address to the Theatre Communications Group National Conference in 1996.[42] Wilson utilizes the vocabulary of a Kwanzaa celebration—testimony, unity with a great ancestral tradition, hard work for the community, and the leadership role of the artist (14). He identifies two sets of pioneers who have given shape and meaning to his life's calling as a playwright—the great dramatists of the Western world including the Greeks, Shakespeare, Shaw, Ibsen, O'Neill, Miller and Williams plus those African Americans represented by his maternal grandfather, Nat Turner, Denmark Vesey, Martin Delaney, Marcus Garvey, and the Honorable Elijah Muhammad (Malcolm X). The first guise taught him about how to express himself through the aesthetic of theatre while the second affirmed the worth of the black human being despite white society's denial.

> The foundation of the American theatre is the foundation of European theatre that begins with the great Greek dramatists.... We embrace the values of that theatre but reserve the right to amend, to explore, to add our African consciousness and our African aesthetic to the art we produce.... We are Americans trying to fulfill our talents. (73)

The Black Power movement of the Sixties he viewed as "the kiln in which I was fired" (14).

---

41 Freedman, 36.
42 August Wilson, "The Ground On Which I Stand," transcript of speech on African American theater by playwright August Wilson, *American Theatre* v. 13 nr. 7 (Sept. 1996), 14–16; 71–74. Citation is from 14.

The ideas of self-determination, self-respect and self-defense that governed my life in the '60s I find just as valid and self-urging in 1996. The need to alter our relationship to the society and to alter the shared expectation of ourselves as a racial group I find of greater urgency now than it was then. (14)

Asserting that race matters because it is the "largest category of identification" (16), Wilson identifies himself as a black American with an African culture. He defines culture, in terms reminiscent of the "life world," as "the behavior patterns, arts, beliefs, institutions and all other products of human work and thought as expressed in a particular community of people." Yet Wilson believes that vestiges of slavery, social segregation, and limited opportunity still exist. When he asks himself why, he cites disparity of economics and privilege that can be demonstrated even in the LORT theatre system, which includes only one black theatre out of sixty-six members. Needless to say, the comment roused the ire of theatre leaders who had fought to include black plays in their repertoire, had been pro-active about minority casting, and had organized outreach to the black community surrounding their theatres. Although he was quick to say that the lack of funding for black theatres was not a complaint, but an advertisement of their plight, Wilson, caught up in his own mission, was probably oblivious to the fundraising difficulties of those very theatres he criticized, as well as to the well-known desire of black actors to tackle the great roles included in Wilson's own list of playwrights from the Greeks through Williams. Wilson instead called for the financial support of black theatres where blacks actors would not be forced to assimilate through colorblind casting or black playwrights to design popular fare for a largely white audience who could afford the tickets. For him, to deny Black Americans their African culture disregards both their history and their values.

Wilson still seeks to "raise the consciousness" of the black community in its continuing quest to define itself in the American context. Just as Malcolm X and Baraka had identified two main groups within the Black community—the house and field Negroes—Wilson talked about two distinct and parallel traditions in black art: entertainment for whites and art for blacks. The first type began in "big house" entertainment (16) for the slaveowner and his guests, reached its apex in the Harlem Renaissance, and found its current counterpart in crossover artists who aim for white consumption. The second incorporated African story, art, song, and dance for blacks in the slave quarters. There the African in America sought to define himself by "invest[ing] his spirit with the strength of his ancestors" (16), through stories which placed him at the "spiritual center" and testified to his existence as a "manifest act of the creator from whom life flowed" and gave his community of "warriors on the cultural battlefield" a survival tool in an environment that treated the black man as property and not as a human being. Wilson claims the second tradition for his own.

Fearing assimilation to white society and the subsequent loss of unique, self-determined values set up by the course of history as well as culture, Wilson refuses to retreat from the progress towards African American identity promoted and achieved by the Black Power movement. As the artist/magician/provocateur, he advocates black theatres where more black playwrights can write specifically out of their experience of the ongoing struggle for recognition of human value without compromise. While Wilson's stance may be called "separatist,"[43] this judgment only admits to a part of the total picture. As a revolutionary, Wilson cannot accept the *status quo*, fights white financial control of the arts, and rejects any notion of the inferiority of minority artists. As a successful playwright, he summons other black playwrights, artists, and actors to gather together because he believes they can mobilize African American energy towards greater political and social change by the shared expression of their journey "from the hull of a ship to self-determining, self-respecting people." For Wilson it is crucial that America recognize the hard work and national loyalty of its black inhabitants, who provided the labor force for the European-led industrial revolution and soldiers for its wars. Simultaneously Wilson offers to meet with other theatre artists, sharing the same craft and dramaturgy, to do the work of extending and developing:

> The ground together:... which our artistic ancestors purchased with their endeavors...with their pursuit of the American spirit and its ideals. (74)

The ground on which both August Wilson and Lillian Hellman stand is definitely American soil. The early political activism seen in Hellman's union building, anti-fascism and articulate defense of the individual's right to speak out for herself/himself as seen in her letter to the House Un-American Activities Committee is as much a part of the American fabric as August Wilson's right to express his demand for recognition and respect for African Americanism as first voiced in the Black Power movement.

When Wilson comments: "I write about the black experience in America and try to explore in terms of the life I know best those things which are common to all cultures,"[44] he expresses what every important dramatist knows. Theatre can examine and transcend social conflict by presenting our

---

[43] Robert Brustein, "Subsidized Separatism," *The New Republic* (8/19/96 & 8/26/96), 39–42.

[44] Preface, August Wilson, *Three Plays*.

differences and simultaneously connecting men to each other on that "common ground" of shared human condition within a shared performance space. The search for a valued human identity allows us all to live a fuller and freer life.

CHAPTER TWO

The Racial Interface:
Construction of Blackness and Whiteness

The task both Hellman and Wilson assume in constructing their dramas based in personal experience is to rectify the inequities they perceived in the treatment of individuals both black and white. Albeit of different eras and of different races, these two dramatists—as members of a citizenry made up of all the peoples of the world, a nation of immigrants tied together by the promise of equal opportunity and democratic freedom—share American expectations of the right to pursue happiness and to affirm one's identity. For both authors, democracy requires a great deal of responsibility on the part of its constituency to forge a national identity inclusive of the individual person and the community from which that individual has sprung. The construction of blackness in Lillian Hellman and its reversal, the construction of whiteness, in August Wilson serve to illuminate the sources of ongoing racial tension and suggest possible solutions.

As a yardstick for comparison of the dramas of Lillian Hellman and August Wilson, Toni Morrison in her groundbreaking *Playing in the Dark: Whiteness and the Literary Imagination* is particularly useful in examining the interracial border.[1] In Morrison's redefinition of American cultural identity through her analysis of a black presence in white fiction, she exposes the hegemony of whiteness, the hierarchical treatment of race, and the shared history of slavery between blacks and whites as a necessary element in the development of American identity—particularly its relationship to the notion of freedom. Slavery with its accompanying and identifying "terror of whiteness," becomes a means of defining the very notion of freedom itself. Toni Morrison recognizes that incoming groups have applied those very repressive elements they left the Old World to escape—poverty, imprisonment, social ostracism, punishment of religious beliefs—to black people in order to bolster a new sense of identity and empowerment among the white peoples of America. From the beginning of the country's settlement, a hegemony of white male property owners had been established, supported by the system of

---

1   Toni Morrison, *Playing in the Dark: Whiteness and the Literary Imagination* (New York: Vintage Books, 1992).

slavery that incorporated at its center the incarceration of a people and the denial of those basic rights promised by the American Constitution and the Bill of Rights. This discrepancy between the promise of the American Dream and its practice inevitably engendered upheaval, tribulation and violence. Sitting on the steps of the Lincoln Memorial while covering the 1963 March on Washington, Hellman witnessed a "remarkable day. Two hundred thousand people come to ask only what they thought had been promised, still calm, pleasant and gay in the face of the one-hundred-year-old refusal."[2]

As playwrights with both politically active pasts and a keen sense of history, Lillian Hellman and August Wilson create dramas for the American commercial stage that cause us to examine ourselves as Americans. Hellman and Wilson expose the racial interface of their respective eras and thereby reveal the success or failure of the American Dream. Both were groundbreakers in regard to interracial relations. The black/white interface they describe is rough-edged due to the novelty of its expression, sometimes resulting in oversimplified or stereotypical presentation of ideas. An examination of the black presence in white drama and its counterpart, white presence in black drama, serves to illuminate the architecture of the new American citizen. In her plays and fictional biographies, Hellman introduces black characters, particularly women, who—while serving their white bosses—simultaneously inculcate them with strong moral values of mutual human respect and accomplishment. Wilson's construction of whiteness, more often expressed in anecdotal references in black conversation than in white characters onstage, contexualizes the black man in American history from the Middle Passage to the present day and allows Wilson to school, question, refute and judge the white man's actions and opinions that have defined the black man in America. Concerned with the psychological slavery still present in those with a heritage of physical slavery and with the economic stratification that continues to relegate the black man to the hold of the ship or, deemed useless, to rough seas—Wilson gives voice to those who have been historyless in the dramatic present and thereby organically onstage constructs a new model of the African American witnessed by both blacks and whites in the audience.

It is important for us today to understand these two authors within the historical context of their own lives. In addition to gender and race, a full generation separates the two. Hellman considers economic problem areas, such as unionization (*Days to Come*) or property ownership for women (*The Little Foxes*), thirty years earlier than Wilson. His later consideration of the

---

2   Lillian Hellman, *An Unfinished Woman*, 265–66.

same subjects as applied to African Americans points to an evolving American identity.

Hellman grew up in the South (New Orleans) with black help and mammy and wrote plays from the Thirties through the early Sixties. She exemplified the youth of the liberated Twenties who worked through the Depression; subscribed to the notion of equal pay for equal work and therefore organized workers; naively believed the Russian system a dream come true, and witnessed American isolationism and the shocking genocide of World War II. She understood capitalism's notion of a free market, but abhorred her own family's exploitation of poor blacks to acquire new wealth—a situation not unfamiliar today in the continued use of Third World cheap labor. The composition of her plays predated the Civil Rights Act and the Black Power movement of the Sixties which served as Wilson's kiln of fire. The integration of lunch counters and schools, sit-ins and marches, and the influx of blacks to the polls only come to figure in Hellman's later biographical fiction.

The memoirs (*An Unfinished Woman, Pentimento, Scoundrel Time* and *Maybe*) draw heavily on her Southern roots and credit two black women, Sophronia and Helen, with the development of Hellman's values:

> Oh, Sophronia, it's you I want back always. It's by you I still so often measure, guess, transmute, translate and act. What strange process made a little girl strain so hard to hear the few words that ever came, made the image of you, true or false, last a lifetime?[3]

Toni Morrison's discussion of "the sycophancy of white identity"[4] in Willa Cather's *Sapphira and the Slave Girl* applies to Hellman's relationship to the black presence expressed in the memoirs. To the only child Lillian, Sophronia was

> the only control I ever recognized, the first and most certain love of my life, She was a tall, handsome, light tan woman—I still have many pictures of the brooding face—who was for me as for so many other Southern white children, the one and certain anchor so needed for the young years.... (24)

Hellman's story of running away from her family to the pink "nigger" boarding house where she declared herself Sophronia Mason's relative, reveals "the interdependent working of power, race, and sexuality in a white woman's battle for coherence" which Morrison saw in Cather (20). However, the perceived mix of love, quest for independence, parental manipulation,

---

3   Lillian Hellman, *An Unfinished Woman*, 256.
4   Morrison, 19.

and first menstruation of an only child viewed through the eyes of an older Hellman is a quest for self that celebrates Sophronia. The child Hellman may be "gathering identity into herself from the wholly available and serviceable lives of Africanist others" (25), but she does not assume that a black woman is simply property, as does the wife who provides the black girl Nancy, a potential rape victim, for an unsatisfied husband. Sapphira's assumption that there is no real family connection between Nancy and her mother because of slavery would never occur to a Hellman whose intimate description of the families of Sophronia, Helen, and Caroline Ducky demonstrates her concern.

In the memoirs, Hellman admits that her attempted dialogue about race was not an easy one. To her praise of her Papa's saving a black girl from rape, Sophronia responds: "Things not going to get themselves fixed by one white man being nice to one nigger girl" (258). When the child Hellman and Sophronia were forced off the bus for sitting up front, Lillian confesses to causing the old woman embarrassment and pain. Hellman's joking with Helen about house niggers and field niggers, while reminiscent of Malcolm X and the period in which Hellman wrote the memoirs, causes enormous friction between the two women:

> "Colored women who cook as well as you do never had a bad time. Not even in slavery.... You were the darlings of every house. What about the others who weren't!"
> She said, "You mean the good house nigger is king boy."
> I said "I mean a house nigger pay no mind to a field hand." (262)

Helen erupts in anger half an hour later.

> "You ain't got no right to talk that way. No right at all. Down South, I cook. Nothing else, just cook. For you, I slave. You made a slave of me and you treat me like a slave...." (262)

Helen then tears up the Hellman's check for royalties from *Toys in the Attic* and says:

> "There. Take it. You think money and presents can pay me, you're wrong."
> I said, "I'm going up to Katonah. That will give you a few days to move out." (262–63)

Hellman eventually perceives that Helen is

> marrow-weary with the struggle to live, bewildered, resentful, sometimes irrational in a changing world where the old, real-pretend love for white people forced her now into open recognition of the hate and contempt she had brought with her from the South.... (251)

Distraught, guilty, and unwilling to face a life without Helen, Hellman returns to New York and finds Helen sitting in a chair with her Bible on the table. They make small talk about Lillian Hellman's hair. Hellman's conclusion is revealing in its brutal honesty about the difficulty of interracial communication:

> We did learn something that day, maybe how much we needed each other, although knowing that often makes relations even more difficult. Our bad times came almost always on the theme of Negroes and whites. The white liberal attitude is, mostly, a well-intentioned fake, and black people should and do think it a sell. But mine was bred, literally from Sophronia's milk, and thus I thought it exempt from such judgments except when I made the jokes about myself. But our bad times did not spring from such conclusions by Helen—they were too advanced, too unkind for her. They came, I think, because she did not think white people capable of dealing with trouble. I was, thus, an intruder, and in the autumn of 1963 she told me so. (264–65)

Helen's declaration that the South had provided a better life for the black man than the North where her children were the victims of poverty and drugs makes Hellman doubly aware and angry over the American "economic system of increasing impurity and injustice."[5] Hellman predates August Wilson in her awareness of America's abuse of cheap labor, of the South as a kind of ancestral homeland for African Americans, and of the black man's residual antagonism and sense of worthlessness when confronted with the white man. Hellman's plays touch upon the link between slavery and economics long before the notion of equal opportunity employment becomes an acceptable mandate.

While Dashiell Hammett criticized her "blackamoor chitchat" in *The Little Foxes*, Hellman's dramatic work goes beyond the clichéd "stepin-fetchit" dialogue of the drama of her time. To be sure, her southern plays all contain their fair share of black house servants who act as butlers, maids, cooks, and housekeepers, but few exist whose function is solely to serve their white bosses. Usually their presence testifies to change or disorder in the household, like Leon the butler in *Autumn Garden*, or their familiarity with the family, like Sophronia in *The Searching Wind* or Joseph in *Watch on the Rhine*. Their treatment by whites reflects on the moral character of the whites themselves. For example, the opening dialogue between Addie and Cal at the top of *The Little Foxes* takes on an upstairs/downstairs quality, but it is a framing device to focus attention on Regina's power in the house and attempt to gain more. If there is anything distinctly Hellman in the scene, it is the outspoken nature of Addie's remark ("You gone stark out of your head?")[6]

---

5   Lillian Hellman, *Pentimento*, 366.
6   Lillian Hellman, *The Little Foxes*, 135.

and Cal's responses which reveal an intimate knowledge of the family they serve and a practiced verbal form of conflict avoidance. Cal's repetition of Zan's expressed love for Addie's delectable frozen fruit creams in turn signifies the affectionate bond between Addie and Zan. While serving coffee and breakfast in Act II, Cal exposes Oscar's small-minded racism when he suggests Oscar give away some of his hunting booty of bobwhite and squirrel to "give every nigger in town a Jesus-party. Most of 'em ain't had no meat since the cotton picking was over. Bet they'd give anything for a little piece of that meat…" (157). Instead of being generous with his haul, Oscar issues a threat: "Cal, if I catch a nigger in this town going shooting, you know what's going to happen" (157). The implied threat of violence against a black man illustrates the fear the white man attempts to inculcate in the black one as well as the white man's fear of what Wilson calls a "nigger with a gun." Long before the Black Power movement advocates taking power into one's own hands, the "terror of whiteness" causes Cal to back off. He will, however, deliver Horace's false message to Manders about the security box because he respects Horace who despises the exploitation of poor blacks and shares Mrs. Bagtry's condemnation of the Hubbards for "overcharging awful interest to ignorant niggers and cheating them on what they bought" (182). While Hellman's servants may exist at the lowest level of Southern society, they are more respectable and likeable than the grasping Hubbards they serve. Addie warns Horace about the horrible possibility of Zan's marriage to Leo, supports the abused and helpless Birdie and watches over Zan's upbringing. Horace's empowerment of a black nanny, Addie, with authority and funds to raise his white daughter in *The Little Foxes* was a dramatic action so revolutionary for the time in which it was written that it was totally omitted in the film version of the play. Instead the screen version brings a white boyfriend to Zan's rescue. Significantly, Hellman has Addie deliver the play's moral message and call to action:

> Yeah, they got mighty well-off cheating niggers. Well, there are people who eat the earth and eat all the people on it like in the Bible with the locusts. And other people who stand around and watch them eat it. *(Softly.)* Sometimes I think it ain't right to stand and watch them do it. (182)

Another Part of the Forest, dealing with the earlier Hubbards in 1880 Bowden, Alabama, presents two black characters onstage—Coralee, who works as Lavinia's maid, and Jake, who carries luggage and serves coffee. Religion connects Coralee and Lavinia. In Act One, they return from the "colored" church to discover Regina in negligée speaking with John Bagtry. Coralee's attitude is one of disapproval. When Marcus refuses to support

Lavinia's request to set up a school for black children, she flees to the kitchen where she is more comfortable with the black folks.

> LAVINIA: Your people are my people. I got to do a little humble service. I lived in sin these thirty-seven years, Coralee.... Now I got to finish with the sin. Now I got to do my mission. And I'll be—I'll do it nice, you know I will. I'll gather the little black children round, and I'll teach them good things. I'll teach them how to read and write, and sing the music notes and—
> CORALEE: *(wearily.)* Oh, Miss Viney. Maybe it's just as well. Maybe they'd be scared of a white teacher coming among them.
> LAVINIA: *(after a pause.)* Scared of me?
> CORALEE: *(wearily.)* No, ma'am. You're right.[7]

By the end of the play, Lavinia reveals Marcus' duplicitous role in the massacre of the Confederate battalion that included the young sons of several people in Bowden. Coralee supports Lavinia's final confrontation with Marcus and thus exceeds Ben's notion that her job is to keep Lavinia out of trouble. Ironically using the historical record of the event in her Bible as evidence against him, Lavinia finally goes off with her black servant Coralee to establish her black school. Even Jake stops serving breakfast so he can take the two women to the sugar boat. Religion here becomes the means of assuaging guilt at the same time it becomes the conduit for education. Some today would consider Lavinia's attitude toward colored people as "forgiving people" patronizing, but she, like Hellman's own mother, enjoyed spending her time with black folk within the Christian church. The combined opportunity to cleanse her sin and build her country school causes her revolution against Marcus.

In contrast to Lavinia, Lillian Hellman takes aim at the male Hubbards who obviously still think of blacks as property a white person can use or abuse at will. Oscar, who never served in the Civil War, is an active member of the Ku Klux Klan who proves his manhood by roughing up carpetbaggers and "upstart niggers." When he attacks Ben for criticizing his girlfriend—the local hooker Laurette Sincee, Marcus suggests he "Go outside and shoot a passing nigger if your blood is throwing clots into your head" (375). However, even Laurette feels she's diminished her already low standing in the community by taking up with one of the Hubbards! Worse is Ben's threat to lynch his own father—an act opposed by Lavinia because a white lynching would lead to a black one!

The Searching Wind presents Sophronia, the housekeeper who's been with the Taney/Hazen family for three generations. Beginning with Musso-

---

7   Lillian Hellman, *Another Part of the Forest,* 351.

lini's invasion of Rome, we see her packing up and condemning the fear-ridden Italians working at the hotel. She says: "They're all scared. I'm sick of it. You come to Europe next summer, you come without me."[8] This Sophronia, unlike most the characters in the play, is totally fearless. She affectionately protects the injured Sam, but can't tolerate the snobbery of Ponette and his wife who resent having to work for the Hazens and blame their Socialist son-in-law (not Hitler!) for their need to leave France. The family patriarch Moses Taney supports the hardworking Sophronia and conveys the truth about her real worth in jest:

> EMILY: Sophronia doesn't like our refugees.
> MOSES: No old American stock likes foreigners. Narrow of us. (275)

While Hellman utilizes those house servants who were part of her extended family experience to explore a Southern biracial world, she alters the real-life models. Lillian's morphine-addicted Aunt Lily loved Peters, her black chauffeur/butler/fancy man in *Pentimento* (363), yet in *Toys in the Attic*, Hellman's focus differs. Henry (the play's Peters) loves the aristocratic Albertine and helps her guide her daughter Lily. Henry even retrieves the drugged girl/child from the life-threatening New Orleans underworld, yet is not afraid to say he'll leave if Lily returns home again instead of staying with her husband. White men, who like Hellman's Uncle Willy, fished up the bayou with black partners and had affairs with part-black Cajun girls or the brutally business-like Uncle Jake, are often either irresponsible or mean-spirited. In *Toys in the Attic*, she attributes both loyalty and generosity to both Gus and Julian. Gus, the black iceman, sticks by his friend Julian, beaten for attempting to help his first love Charlotte Warkins, Henry's cousin in a real estate scheme. His sister, the white spinster Carrie, jealously condemns Julian's wife Lily as "a crazy little whore...the daughter of a woman who keeps a nigger fancy man," and betrays her brother by manipulating Lily into revealing both Julian's location and his wife's mixed blood to the gangster Cyrus Warkins. The brutal retaliation forces Julian back into dependency upon his sisters. Morrison, who examines the white man's association of blackness with primitive sexuality and breeding animals, would concur with Hellman's linkage of frustrated sexuality and racism in white behavior.

In summary, the presence of black characters in Hellman's plays testifies to the dignity of the African American. While it is true that all of her black characters are domestic help, not all of them simply serve coffee, carry luggage, or gossip. Instead, the Addies, Sophronias and Henrys of the Southern

---

8   Lillian Hellman, *The Searching Wind*, 283.

world indelibly shape those whites in their charge. Possessing enormous moral stature, Hellman's black characters represent the tip of a societal iceberg that can only be fully revealed when an African American with the talent and skill of August Wilson takes us into the neighborhood where the African American odyssey comes alive.

August Wilson constructs whiteness in his dramas to set into relief both the *status quo* position of the black man and simultaneously to indicate a road towards the affirmation of cultural identity and social betterment in a nation touting "liberty and justice for all." While Wilson introduces white characters onstage in only two of his plays to date—*Ma Rainey's Black Bottom* and *Joe Turner's Come and Gone*—his work as a general rule presents whiteness in an anecdotal fashion through stories and comments about white behavior. This narrative mode reflects the attitude of black characters towards the white man—revealing African American history from the Middle Passage up to the time of the particular drama's decade, the powerful influence of white thinking and values on the black man, and the continuation of an economic exploitation that inevitably explodes in violence inside and outside the black community policed by a law enforcement system prejudiced in favor of whites.

Wilson presents black characters who see themselves existing at the bottom of the socioeconomic scale, earning little and sharing housing to survive, often still dependent on the white man to provide employment or necessary goods for sale, and policed or jailed if he fails to comply with white notions of proper behavior. At the hands of the white man, the black man assumes those same elements the Old World offered to America's first immigrants—"poverty, prison, social ostracism, and not infrequently, death." Until power, control of one's own destiny, replaces the "powerlessness felt before the gates of class, caste, and cunning persecution,"[9] violence is sure to erupt. Wilson, forged in the kiln of the Black Power movement, sees his theatre, in Morrison terms, as "a once-in-a-lifetime opportunity not only to be born again but to be born again in new clothes, as it were. The setting would provide raiments of self. This second chance could even benefit from the mistakes of the first."[10] Hence, the African American must know his past to find his identity and his future as a citizen. Wilson's Pittsburgh locale provides a safe haven for open discussion among blacks for blacks and whites and an opportunity to stop the ongoing practice of "stacking niggers," as Holloway puts it, the continuing financial exploitation of blacks. Wilson at-

---

9   Morrison, 35.
10   *Ibid.*, 34.

tempts a redefinition of American cultural identity inclusive of an architecture for a "new black man."

Often in Wilson's plays, the black man will ape the white man's values, either in his demand for equal rights and independence or in the devaluation or commercialization of his African American heritage. He, like Seth or Martha Pentecost or Rose, will choose white Christianity over the African spiritual traditions of the Yoruba or the herbalist/conjurer's link to nature. He, like Levee or Floyd, will sell his music for fancy clothes or Cadillacs. He will even turn on his own community when denied the material accoutrements of American consumer culture (Levee vs. Toledo) or when threatened by the selfish greed which could lead to the extinction of his own race (King Hedley vs. Floyd). As long as the sense of powerlessness/worthlessness exists, the black man will turn against his own in the sheer effort of survival.

Wilson sees the solution to the African American identity dilemma in gaining knowledge of African traditions and African American history coupled with respect for the person, family, and community. He advocates an appreciation for uniqueness and excellence in both music (the blues) and athletics and dignifies hard work as a means to owning property (Malcolm X's stress on land) and developing one's own business to guarantee independence in the context of white, capitalistic America. To combat the sense of powerlessness or worthlessness once closely associated with physical bondage, Wilson presents men who succeed as independent citizens as well as those whose low self-esteem, poverty, and ignorance lead them to crime, death, and imprisonment. A history only too familiar to many African Americans, but one that can be changed.

Certainly Wilson's decidedly human world contains people who, in searching out the new land, run after adventure (like Lyons or Wining Boy) or cash (Floyd, Prophet Samuel, the Numbers runners, and even Undertaker West) at the expense of their brothers. His blues musicians testify to the identity and history of the entire race rather than the importance of a nuclear family, a notion made unfamiliar because of slavery's fragmentation. Above all, Wilson preempts white clichés about blacks as shiftless, lazy, uneducated, pagan, primitive, superstitious, promiscuous, and violent, with dramas about responsible, talented African Americans, his warrior spirits. Whites, like those who burned Memphis's family home and gang-raped his mother, demonstrate the very attributes they project onto blacks. Wilson defeats the very labeling that keeps black people down. He tells us of whites whose exploitation of blacks relegates them to the bottom of a democratic society and simultaneously illuminates the high cost of a shattering diaspora upon the black man's sense of worth as a human being and his crucial search for identity in a society where he was once designated property. Wilson uses examples of white assertions of power to insure their own freedom at the expense of the black man. In so doing, Wilson exposes effective methods for the black man to claim his independence—despite post-Abolition "freedom" restricted by poverty, lack of education, the absence of a family support system, the corruption of Reconstruction, and the harshness of share-cropping and dislocation, for both Southern blacks and whites, to the North. For Wilson, the black man himself becomes a property owner who like Boy Willie takes possession of land in the South once worked by his forebears, runs his own restaurant like Memphis in *Two Trains Running,* and plans to return to the South to reclaim his land and avenge his mother's gang-rape, unites a fragmented family like Rose in *Fences* or accepts and furthers a spiritual journey from the Middle Passage to the present like Herald Loomis in *Joe Turner's Come and Gone.* Wilson goes further and tackles slavery's physical and psychological invasion of the black man's psyche and its subsequent devastation. His courageous Boy Willie finally confronts the murdering ghost of slaveowner Sutter who still wields a terrifying power that extends to a northern city in the Thirties. Only Berniece's calling upon the African ancestral spirits, not white wannabe Avery's Christian exorcism, can defeat this evil spirit.

White economic exploitation of blacks—seen in Hendricks' low pay for Sterling, Red Carter's less than negotiated Chicago fee, Jeremy's guitar contest, Lubin's low sharecropping salary for a family of 11 kids, Joe Turner's seven-year impressment of black chain gangs, Lutz's treatment of Hambone—is rampant. Coming from an agrarian African and Southern background, migrating illiterate and unskilled blacks face unemployment. Consequently it is hugely difficult for black men to attain credit to purchase furniture or homes (Troy) or loans to set up an independent black business (Seth Holly's tinsmithing). Pawnshops, numbers, welfare, rooming houses all testify to poverty and frustration. Whites own property, lend money, and control the legal/justice system. Wilson shows the solution in a black man who runs his own business and, like Memphis, is smart enough to hire a white lawyer who knows how to work the system to get Memphis the best price for his diner.

Social ostracism is glaringly apparent in ghettoes where white businesses move out of the Hill District, jitney cabs take black people where yellow cabs won't go, and even a successful black undertaker like West waits years to have glass instead of wood boards in his windows. Ironically, West hires Mason, a white ex-policeman, to guard his mortuary with a shotgun; while another white policeman shoots Poochie in the back during the attempted

robbery. Imprisonment—whether it be in the Parchman Farm, the workhouse, a Chicago jail, or the Pittsburgh penitentiary—is an experience shared
by Herald Loomis, Troy, Bono, Crawley, Lymon, Boy Willie and Doaker, to
name a few. For Wilson, it takes a warrior spirit like Troy Maxson, an ex-con
jailed for poverty-induced burglary and killing, to fight for and gain a promotion in union ranks from garbage collector to driver—despite quivelling
from another black man, Brownie.

> TOLEDO: As long as the colored man look to white folks to put the crown on
> what he say...as long as he looks to white folks for approval...then he ain't never
> gonna find out who he is and what he's about. He's just gonna be about what white
> folks want him to be about. That's one sure thing.[11]

What do white folks want the black man to be about and how does the
black man view the white? To begin our textual examination of Wilson's
construction of whiteness onstage, it is particularly fruitful to start with the
only two plays in which white characters actually appear. In *Ma Rainey's
Black Bottom*, there are three white characters: the record producers, Irv and
Sturdyvant, plus a policeman. We are on the white man's turf, not the Hill
District of Pittsburgh, but a Chicago recording studio owned and operated by
white men. While Irv, Ma's manager "prides himself on his knowledge of
blacks and his ability to deal with them" (11), Sturdyvant is "preoccupied
with money and insensitive to black performers" (11). Paramount to their
discussion is Sturdyvant's mandate to "keep Ma in line" because he won't
tolerate any of her "Mother of the Blues bullshit" (11–12). He also recognizes that Levee's jazzier dance music would appeal to big city buyers as
opposed to Ma's Southern following. Whatever the approach, the objective
for the white men is still to make as much profit from black music as possible
and retain their position of power in a social hierarchy left over from slavery.
The racial interface is still primarily an economic one. The producers refuse
to provide even basic creature comforts like heat in the studio or Coke to
drink and relegate the black musicians, doubly cursed for being both blacks
and artists, to the basement. As if they were penned animals, Irv's job is to
"get them fed" (14) so the recording session can occur as soon as possible
and in the least expensive fashion. Ultimately the white man still treats the
black man as property, whether the crop is cotton or music.

On the other hand, these black musicians in 1927 (well before the black
entrepreneurship later expressed in Motown Records), still look to the white
men for employment, a holdover from the days of slavery. The black char-

---

11   August Wilson, *Ma Rainey's Black Bottom*, 29.

acters in the play associate wealth, power, punishment, death and even literacy with the white man. In control of jobs, property and the justice system, the white man is the supreme predator with legal power to police and to punish with jail terms. Stories from the past tell of whites gang-raping Levee's mother and lynching his father, an "uppity nigger" who owned his own land, or of carpetbagger Eliza Cotter escaping a murder conviction because he plays along with the white judge. The play's present action gives us a white policeman refusing to believe that Ma can own her own car and charging her with assault and battery when a ruckus occurs over a white cabby's refusal to haul colored folks. Significantly, Wilson gives Irv the authority to identify Ma and pay off the policeman. The policeman's judgment that everything's okay "as long as someone is responsible for them" implies that blacks, like children, are incapable of taking care of themselves. Nor can Ma stay in a white hotel or be invited to white homes, even if she is a musical star. Even the Christian god refuses to help the Bible-toting Reverend Gates forced to dance by a threatening group of white men.

> The problem ain't with the white man. The white man knows you just a leftover. Cause he the one who done the eating and he made history out of. Done went and filled the white man's belly and now he's full and tired and wants you to get out the way and let him be by himself. Now, I know what I'm talking about. And if you wanna find out, you just ask Mr. Irvin what he had for supper yesterday. And if he's an honest white man...which I asking for a whole heap of a lot...he'll tell you he done ate your black ass and if you please I'm full up with you...so go and get off the plate and let me at something else.
> ....
> See, we's the leftovers. The colored man is the leftovers. Now, wha's the colored man gonna do with himself? That' what we waiting to find out. But first we gotta know we the leftovers. Now, who knows that? You find me a nigger that knows that and I'll turn any which away you want me to. I'll bend over for you. You ain't gonna find that. And that's what the problem is. (47)

To fill in African American history and values, Wilson appoints Toledo, who knows that if the black man continues to think as a slave, he'll be treated like one. He also sees that simply accepting the white man's prejudices and material values provides no solution to finding African American self-respecting identity if it means denigrating African American distinctiveness. The inability to transcribe music, or mistaking a pair of Florsheim shoes bought with money won in a crap game as marks of success, are just as primitive as wearing a bone through your nose.

> TOLEDO: We done sold Africa for the price of tomatoes. We done sold ourselves to the white man in order to be like him. Look at the way you dressed.... That

ain't African. That the white man. We trying to be just like him. We done sold who
we are in order to become someone else. We's imitation white men. (24)

Unfortunately, Levee doesn't understand that he can't "Make the white man
respect me!" if he does not respect himself first. Wilson sees the commodification of music and adjustment to white tastes in Levee's dance arrangements as a compromise doomed to failure. Levee sells his soul to the white
devil. His dependency on Sturdyvant to buy his songs and hire his band indicates that he is "spooked" by the white man. His fear allows Sturdyvant to
devalue his music to the level of five bucks per song. The subsequent frustration and humiliation lead him to attack Toledo, who exacerbates the situation by stepping on his treasured Florsheim shoes. Tragically, Levee murders
one of his own, instead of the white man he truly fears, the one who killed
his smiling father.

To provide the solution to the black man's dilemma, Wilson introduces
his female warrior spirit—Ma Rainey. She knows the reason for the blues is
to "reconnect" African Americans with each other, to share "life talking"
through a unique form of musical expression no white man could create. She
defies Sturdyvant's attempt to tell her how to do her song, because she understands he's only interested in making money. She demands her rights and
her money, schools Sylvester in overcoming his stutter, and forces the producers to allow Sylvester to record the introduction. Ma knows the unique
value of the blues and charges accordingly. She won't sign a release until
Sylvester is paid because she knows that the white man will treat her like an
old whore or a "dog in an alley" (65) once he's got what he wants—music
that for the white man is simply property used to make a profit. Ma refuses to
sell her soul to the devil (34–35), to the white man whose presence provokes
divisiveness among blacks [Irv blames Levee for the failure to record Ma's
take (71–73)] and the tragic murder of Toledo (90–91).

In summation, August Wilson depicts an American world torn apart by
racism—a world in which whites continue to treat black men as less than
human, as a means of making money through their music. It is a world of
impending violence in which white men try to keep black men in subservient
positions. Taxidrivers refuse to pick up blacks; policemen cry assault and
battery; cracker farmers rape a black woman because her husband is a landowner; a white judge acquits a black murderer who works for a white carpetbagger; and a white God fails to protect a colored minister. At the same time,
Wilson demands his African Americans to be more than "imitation white
men." He wants the new black man and woman to know their history, name
their gods, respect their own music, work for equitable pay, and even own
their own homes. Ma Rainey is a role model for an independent and respon-

sible African American identity. In *Joe Turner's Come and Gone*, August Wilson chooses yet another historical figure who immediately locates us in a specific time period. Where Ma Rainey transported us to the blues capital of 1927 Chicago, Joe Turner, the white Governor's brother infamous for impressing free Negroes into chain gangs as unpaid laborers for seven years, takes us back to 1911 Tennessee.[12] In essence, Joe Turner's behavior continues slavery's oppression of blacks by using the state government system to provide free labor during Reconstruction. Unlike Ma's independent spirit, Herald Loomis is totally lost. He is a "leftover from history," a man come to Pittsburgh in search of himself and the wife he lost when Joe Turner trapped him. To help Loomis find himself and his place in the world, Wilson provides him with two guides, one black (Bynum, an African healer) and one white (Rutherford Selig, the "People Finder").

In contrast to *Ma Rainey's Black Bottom*, Wilson introduces a white character onstage to opposite effect in *Joe Turner's Come and Gone*. Selig, whose German name means holy or blessed, reunites blacks separated from their families by slavery and northward migration. Selig is a most unusual and daring creation.

> That idea of people leaving each other, of people being separated—there has to be someone who wants to heal them and bind them together. So that's how the idea of the Binder came about. I gave him the name Bynum.... The People Finder is almost the same concept, but it's a White application of it. Rutherford Selig is a peddler of pots and pans. He travels about knocking on people's doors, and as a result he's the only one who knows where everybody lives. So if the people were looking for someone, it's only logical they would ask Selig. I don't think he called himself the People Finder—this is something the people of the community called him...he's not evil at all. In fact, he's performing a very valuable service for the community. The fact that his father was a "People Finder" who worked for the plantation bosses and caught runaway slaves has no bearing on Selig's character. That was a job. That was something he did and got paid for. His grandfather was a "Bringer" working on a slave ship. Selig doesn't make any apologies for any of this. It's not his fault. It was his grandfather's job. It was hard work. His grandfather got married and had some kids. This contact with Blacks, of being paid for performing some service that involved Blacks, has been going on in his family for a long time. Selig is the guy who opens up a hardware store in a Black community. He's got a long history of involvement.[13]

Selig is not only the connector/conduit for families shattered twice by slavery and northward migration, but he also becomes the bearer of black history. Selig says to Loomis:

---

[12] Kim Powers, "An Interview with August Wilson," *Theater* (Fall/Winter, 1984), 40.
[13] *Ibid.*, 53.

We been finders in my family for a long time. Bringers and finders. My great-grandaddy used to bring Nigras across the ocean on ships. That wasn't no easy job either. Sometimes the winds would blow so hard you'd think the hand of God was set against the sails. But it set him well in pay and he settled in this new land and found him a wife of good Christian charity with a mind for kids and the like and well here I am, Rutherford Selig. You're in good hands, mister. Me and my daddy have found plenty Nigras. My daddy, rest his soul, used to find runaway slaves for the plantation bosses. He was the best there was at it. Jonas B. Selig. Had him a reputation stretched clean across the country. After Abraham Lincoln give you all Nigras your freedom papers and with you all looking all over for each other...we started finding Nigras for Nigras. Of course, it don't pay as much. But the People Finding business ain't so bad.[14]

Egalitarian in his treatment of Selig, Wilson does not blame a man who left home because his wife wished him dead and now attempts to rectify the destructive effect of slavery by reconnecting those families who have lost each other and helping them to reassemble their lives. If anything, Selig's continuous history sets into relief the central character's dilemma as a man who has lost his history and family, a man who has lost all sense of identity and self-worth at the hands of white Joe Turner. Ma Rainey would agree with Bynum's assessment: "when a man forgets his song he goes off in search of it...till he find out he's got it with him all the time. That's why I can tell you one of Joe Turner's niggers. 'Cause you forgot how to sing your song" (70).

In the process of that search, Loomis witnesses white bones rising up out of the ocean, taking on black flesh and walking up on the land. "This is his connection with the ancestors, the Africans who were lost during the Middle Passage and were thrown overboard. He is privileged to witness this because he needs most to know who he is."[15] Wilson here extends his use of whiteness to the metaphorical level in that Loomis' vision is one of being born again as black flesh brings old dead "white" bones to life.

Additionally, Loomis also confronts whiteness in the form of Christianity, harkening back to Wilson's treatment of the white man's god failing Reverend Gates in *Ma Rainey*. Captured by Joe Turner when he, as a deacon in the Abundant Life Church, tried to preach to a bunch of gamblers, Loomis loses all respect for the white man's god, the "Holy Ghost" mentioned in the juba ceremony. Instead, he insists on his own freedom to bleed for himself and not let Jesus bleed for him at the end of the play. While Selig helps him find his wife Martha Pentecost, Loomis rejects her offer of salvation through Jesus.

---

[14]   August Wilson, *Joe Turner's Come and Gone*, 41.
[15]   Powers, 54.

Great big old white man...your Mr. Jesus Christ. Standing there with a whip in one hand and tote board in another; and them niggers swimming in a sea of cotton. And he counting. He tallying up the cotton. "Well, Jeremia...what's the matter, you ain't picked but two hundred pounds of cotton today? Gotto put you on half rations." And Jeremia go back and lay up there on his half rations and talk about what a nice man Mr. Jesus Christ is 'cause he give him salvation after he die. Something wrong here. Something don't fit right! (93)

The metaphorical link between the whiteness of cotton and the whiteness of Christ is unmistakable. Loomis becomes his own savior as Wilson, in a fascinating use of blood fetishization, turns blood into a metaphor for purification. Loomis slashes himself with his own blood and discovers that he can stand, finds his "song of self sufficiency" and accepts "responsibility for his own presence in the world." He is "free to soar at last" (94). Loomis stops the "hand of God" that set the wind against those slave ship sails in Selig's description of the Middle Passage.

As in *Ma Rainey*, various other white characters—tradesmen, employers, salesmen—are mentioned by anecdote. They, too, illustrate that the black/white interface is mostly an economic one with whites policing blacks. Whites continue to view the black man as a source of cheap labor, often exploited by small racketeers like those demanding "protection money" from Jeremy's road gang and thereby keeping the threat of death or unemployment alive. Unfortunately, Jeremy, recently from the South, looks to the white man for work, just as slavery created a dependency upon the white man for employment. Yet the white man cannot distinguish one black man from the next. Molly tells Jeremy: "You can go on back down there tomorrow and go back to work if you want. They won't even know who you is" (64–65) Jeremy corroborates her statement with the story of the music contest in which the white man couldn't differentiate between Jeremy, Old Hooter, and Bobo. Instead, he gives the three musicians twenty-five cents total in a small bit of exploitation reminiscent of Sturdyvant's five dollars apiece for Levee's songs. The difference, Bynum tells Jeremy, is that Seefus's place provides a community "where the music at. That's where the people at. The people down there making music and enjoying themselves. Some things is worth taking the chance going to jail about" (18). Yet as soon as Jeremy participates in the life of the black community, he does get jailed or fined for drinking on his payday. Whites still manipulate law enforcement to police the black man. Bertha says: "You know the police do that. Figure there's too many people out on the street they take some of them off" (13). Physical control and puritanical suppression of perceived loose behavior converge.

Against the white misperception of irresponsibility on the part of black males, Wilson sees Seth Holly as an "honest picture of the black male in

America. The idea of responsibility is crucial because, I believe, white Americans basically see black males as irresponsible, which I think is incorrect."[16] A tinsmith by trade, Seth is a Northern free man whose parents and grandparents had never been slaves. He owns the boarding house and represents the urban, not agrarian, part of the black experience. Like the white man, Seth is a property owner. However, like many Americans who want a business of their own, Seth dreams of opening up his own shop instead of working for Mr. Oloski at night and making pots and pans for Selig to sell. "Get me four or five fellows and teach them how to make pots and pans. One man making ten pots is five men making fifty" (206). However, the white man controls the purse and makes the opportunity to run one's own business a difficult one for a responsible black man. The rub lies in the next-to-impossible situation of a getting a loan whether it be from Mr. Johnson the banker or Sam Green the moneylender. The bank won't grant the loan unless Seth signs over his boarding house as collateral. The risk of losing his home and his independence is too great.

While Selig helps Loomis discover his place in African American history, find his wife and ultimately take responsibility for his spiritual journey, church-going Seth gets caught in the middle as he still struggles both with African religious notions (Bynum) and white-controlled lending institutions. Both men strive for the freedom found in a sure sense of selfhood within the context of America. The black man's story is intimately tied to that of the white man.

> Identity means understanding your political history as well as your social history. It means understanding that you come from a long line of honorable people who were slaves. Writing our own history has been a very valuable tool, because if we're going to be pointed toward a future, we must know our past. This is so basic and simple yet it's a thing that Africans in America disregard. For instance, the fact of slavery is something that blacks do not teach their kids—they do not tell their kids that at one time we were slaves. That is the most crucial and central thing to our presence here in America. It's nothing to be ashamed of. Why is it, after spending hundreds of years in bondage, that blacks in America do not once a year get together and celebrate the Emancipation and remind ourselves of our history?[17]

Wilson suggests that Loomis and all those searching for their identity in a nation so diverse need both a Selig and a Bynum to guide the way.

---

16   David Savran, In Their Own Words: Contemporary American Playwrights (New York: TCG Inc., 1988), 298.

17   August Wilson in Alan Nadel, *May All Your Fences Have Gates: Essays on the Drama of August Wilson* (Iowa City: U of Iowa P, 1994), 295–96.

By 1957, the hard-won victories of the European immigrants had solidified the industrial might of America. War had been confronted and won with new energies that used loyalty and patriotism as its fuel. Life was rich, full, and flourishing. The Milwaukee Braves won the World Series, and the hot winds of change that would make the sixties a turbulent, racing, dangerous, and provocative decade had not yet begun to blow full.[18]

While the European may have seized control of America's industrial wealth and power earlier on, the black man found himself heir to veteran's benefits from World War II which included rights hitherto promised, but largely denied him in practice. The black man could now become a property owner, claim the right to an education and medical/dental care, and participate in professional athletics (baseball!) in a manner denied to him prior to the war. Perhaps not the sixties hot winds of change, but the breezy promise of opportunity inflated black hopes at the same time as it reawakened the myopic bitterness attendant upon past oppression. Hence, there is a legacy of contradiction in the very intertwining of whiteness, economics and the American notion of freedom. Morrison's concept of slavery as the "heart of darkness" at the center of American democracy takes on new mutations (128).

In no other character has August Wilson imbued these contradictions more than that of Troy Maxson. He is the personification of this breach between promise and practice regarding freedom, the disjunction amplified by World War II.

> TROY: Don't nobody wanna be locked up, Rose. What you wanna lock him up for? Man go over there and fight the war...messing around with them Japs, get half his head blown off...and they give him a lousy three thousand dollars. And I had to swoop down on that.... That's the only way I got a roof over my head...cause of that metal plate. If my brother didn't have that metal plate in his head...I wouldn't have a pot to piss in or a window to throw it out of.... (128)

Knowledge of the African American past becomes both a burden and an incentive when Troy and his friend Bono adjust to change. Bono says to Troy:

> I hear you tell it. Me and Lucille was staying down there on Logan Street. Had two rooms with the outhouse in the back.... To this day I wonder why in the hell I ever stayed down there for six long years. But see, I didn't know I could do no better. I thought only white folks had inside toilets and things. (110)

Money becomes the mechanism for advancement and independence. Troy knows that white folks have the money so he jokes: "I know who your banker is. Mellon don't need that money bad as Lucille want that refrigera-

---

[18] August Wilson, *Fences,* 103, 104.

tor" (159). Bono boasts that "When it comes to my money...I'm right as fireworks on the Fourth of July" (159). Money, freedom, and whiteness intertwine in the American context.

On the one hand, Troy can't forget his background of poverty as one of eleven sharecropper's kids or his imprisonment for theft and murder in a desperate attempt to support Lyons' mother or his rejection as a black baseball player in pro ball before Jackie Robinson broke the color barrier. Troy holds tenaciously to the usual stereotypes about the white hegemony: Lubin the white landowner's financial exploitation of his father, a white prison system and local police which curb blacks with payoffs such as that required for Gabe's "disturbing the peace," raids on Seefus' place, Lyons' incarceration in the workhouse or ostracism from professional sports despite obvious athletic ability. He is not able to hear Rose's admonition on Cory's behalf. She says: "Times have changed since you was playing baseball, Troy. That was before the war. Times have changed a lot since them.... They got lots of colored boys playing ball now. Baseball and football" (112). Instead he fails to scc positive white efforts towards his son and rejects the white recruiter and high school coach who campaign for Cory's football skills as a means of getting a college education. Like many of his generation, black and white, Troy believes work in the trades will provide a sufficiently good future. Ultimately, Troy's misuse of Gabe will drive Cory out of the house into a career once reserved for the white man—that of a Marine.

On the other hand, Troy learns to play according to the white man's rules when he successfully negotiates a promotion in the union ranks from garbage collector to truck driver, despite his illiteracy and lack of a license. Wilson also notes that Troy operates on a white man's advice to file a complaint and talk with the union commissioner to assure his promotion even though another black man, Brownie, asserting seniority, opposes his advancement. Troy's too proud to slink around like Brownie, who stupidly thinks he's hiding a stolen watermelon from the eyes of the white man and resorts to backstabbing his black brother. Yet, Troy too betrays his own brother to gain independence or additional funds to carry on with Alberta. First he takes advantage of Gabe's veteran's benefits to buy a house, thereby becoming a property owner—something not possible in the days of slavery. When he can no longer accept Gabe's attempts at independence in moving to Pearl's or earning a livelihood selling vegetables culled from the strip or paying his brother's fines, Troy signs Gabe over to a government-operated residential medical facility and keeps a percentage of the funds. Troy, in essence, enslaves his brother to insure his own independence. Unlike Toni Morrison's example of whites using blacks to bolster up their own sense of new world identity, blacks turn on blacks. Troy's ex-con perspective confuses economic and spiritual freedom and tragically affects the Maxson family. His betrayal, like Brownie's, points out the divisiveness the rush for money causes within the black community.

For Troy, the white man is still Death in white robes (114). He knows how to extract whatever money or valuables, like the meat in Pope's stew, the black man possesses. Wilson even comically personifies Hertz-berger/Glickman, whose credit plan for furniture extorts much more than the goods are worth, as the devil himself. Troy knows, unlike Cory who wants to buy a TV on the installment plan, that debt can take away his house. Therein lies his fear of whiteness. Troy is not different from Seth Holly or Ma Rainey's musicians in his knowledge that cash, not credit, guarantees the black man ownership and thereby a sense of independence and worth. Yet unlike them, he chooses to work collecting garbage for the white man rather than go out on his own. For a man who knows homelessness firsthand, ex-pressed in his railroad lullaby to his baby girl by Alberta, maintaining a roof is of paramount importance to his sense of identity and self-worth.

> —Woman…I do the best I can do. I come in here every Friday. I carry a sack of potatoes and a bucket of lard. You all line up at the door with you hands out. I give you the lint from my pockets. I give you my sweat and my blood. I ain't got no tears. I done spent them. We go upstairs in that room at night…and I fall down on you and try to blast a hole into forever. I get up Monday morning…find my lunch on the table. I go out. Make my way. Find my strength to carry me through to the next Friday. *(Pause.)* That's all I got, Rose. That's all I got to give. I can't give nothing else. (138)

The deadening economic treadmill pushes him to seek relief in Alberta and shatters his marriage. Moreover his new job may allow Troy to be as lazy as the white man sitting around and reading the paper (45), but it separates him from his old friends and relegates him to picking up white men's garbage in Greentree. Money does not solve his loneliness. Ultimately, his salvation lies in his reunification with his own African American community in death. Rose's explanation of his father to Cory, the duet of Raynell and Cory sing-ing old dog Blue out of slavery to the Promised Land, and Gabe's African dance of brotherhood, unite Troy with the ancestors, after the Christian trum-pet fails to sound. Understanding leads to forgiveness and to celebration. Raynell's garden metaphorically blows life into tomorrow.

> When the sins of our fathers visit us
> We do not have to play host.
> We can banish them with forgiveness
> As God, in His Largeness and Laws. (95)

While property ownership plays a major part in *The Piano Lesson* as well, Wilson clearly utilizes the land/piano opposition to expose black/white history and its relationship to freedom on economic and spiritual levels. Boy Willie, imbued with Wilson's black power philosophy of the Sixties, declares:

> See now...I'll tell you something about me. I done strung along and strung along. Going this way and that. Whatever way would lead me to a moment of peace. That's all I want. To be as easy with everything. But I wasn't born to that. I was born to a time of fire.
>
> The world ain't wanted no part of me. I could see that since I was about seven. The world say it's better off without me. See, Berniece accept that. She trying to come up to where she can prove something to the world. Hell, the world a better place cause of me. I don't see it like Berniece. I got a heart that beats here and it beats just as loud as the next fellow's. Don't care if he black or white. Sometime it beats louder. When it beats louder, then everybody can hear it. Some people get scared of that. Like Berniece. Some people get scared to hear a nigger's heart beating. They think you ought to lay low with that heart. Make it beat quiet and go along with everything the way it is. But my mama ain't birthed me for nothing. So what I got to do: I got to mark my passing on the road. Just like you write on a tree, "Boy Willie was here."
>
> ....
>
> That's all I'm trying to do with that piano. Trying to put my mark on the road. Like my daddy done. My heart say for me to sell that piano and get me some land so I can make a life for myself to live in my own way. Other than that I ain't thinking about nothing Berniece got to say.[19]

Recognizing that Berniece's denial of her African American legacy comes from a belief that blacks reside at the "bottom of life"—even below Troy's collecting garbage for white people—Wilson, in Boy Willie's voice, asserts the worth of America's black citizens to eliminate an inherited slave mentality once and for all. Above all, he forces the audience to confront the African American residual "terror of whiteness" and defeat Sutter's ghost.

> If you teach that girl that she living at the bottom of life, she's gonna grow up and hate you.... If you believe that's where you at then you gonna act that way. If you act that way then that's where you gonna be. It's as simple as that. Ain't no mystery to life. I don't know how you come to believe that stuff. Crawley didn't think like that. He wasn't living at the bottom of life. Papa Boy Charles and Mama Ola wasn't living at the bottom of life. You ain't never heard them say nothing like that. They would have taken a strap to you if they heard you say something like that.... That sound like something Avery would say. Avery think cause the white man give him a turkey for Thanksgiving that makes him better than everybody else. That's gonna raise him out of the bottom of life. I don't need nobody to give me a turkey. I can

---

[19] August Wilson, *The Piano Lesson*, 92–94.

get my own turkey. All you have to do is get out my way. I'll get me two or three turkeys…. (92–94)

Wilson also captures a time of flux when the old white/black relationship is undergoing change. To be sure, Wilson shows whites in control as operators of a prison system including Parchman Farm where both Lymon's father and Lymon had served their time, or as the sheriff's patrol who murder Crawley for stealing. As in *Ma Rainey*, the white man attempts to co-opt Black culture by buying his musical instruments, recording Wining Boy's boogie woogie or Joe Herrin's paying him fifty cents a day in his old age. However, in 1937 Boy Willie can actually buy the land of his father's slave-owner, if he can put the funds together. Even Avery may receive a loan from the white moneylenders to build his church. Moreover, Berniece's refusal to sell the piano to help Avery build his Christian church or Boy Willie to buy the old Stovall place announces that African American culture is no longer for sale. Now the white man fails in his "contest to see who can buy the most" watermelons (59). He deserts poor Southern farm land in a rush for Northern profits in the manufacture of soda fountain equipment or Pittsburgh steel, yet there is no escape for poverty of spirit.

Retribution follows the trail of whiteness. The Ghosts of the Yellow Dog, obviously Boy Willie's allies, take revenge and throw their white killers down wells, including the former slaveowner Sutter himself. As for Sutter's ghost, he may travel northward to haunt those black folks who once existed at his beck and call, but they are no longer content to live at "the bottom of life." Applying the anecdote about Reverend C.L. Thompson's failure to bring his puppy back to life and his subsequent cat killing, Willie confronts the Death identified with whiteness whether it be Sutter's ghost or Berniece with Crawley's gun. Boy Willie learns the lesson of protest and action. He discovers the "power of death":

> See, a nigger that ain't afraid to die is the worse kind of nigger for the white man. He can't hold that power over you. That's what I learned when I killed that cat. I got the power of death too. I can command him. I can call him up. The white man don't like to see that. He don't like you to stand up and look him square in the eye and say, "I got it too." Then he got to deal with you square up.[20]

Wilson starves out Sutter's hungry ghost, who appears every time there's an attempt to move and sell the piano to the white man or any disruption of the Doaker family's connection to their ancestors and thereby their African American spiritual legacy.

---

[20]   August Wilson, *The Piano Lesson*, 88.

Yet the play does not end with Boy Willie's confrontation with the powerful, fear-instilling whiteness, but with the celebratory reunion of Berniece joining Willie in the battle by calling up the strength of her African American spiritual ancestry. Solidarity eliminates the trauma of brother/sister conflict and the need for white Christianity evidenced by Avery's futile exorcism. Berniece does let "her color show"; she declares her uniqueness and simultaneously her membership in the African American community. Hence, whiteness defined by skin color, power upheld by the threat of violence and property ownership, must bow to blackness claiming the common inheritance of humanity, the promise portended in the 4th of July piano stealing.

> BOY WILLIE: You ought to mark down on the calendar the day that Papa Boy Charles brought that piano into the house. You ought to mark that day down and draw a circle around it...and every year when it come up throw a party. Have a celebration. If you did that she [Maretha] wouldn't have no problem in life. She could walk around here with her head held high. I'm talking about a big party!
>
> ....
>
> Invite everybody! Mark that day down with a special meaning. That way she know where she at in the world. (91)

Freedom lies in the acceptance of cultural identity and history and in the black man's secure belief in his value as a human being.

> If the train don't hurry
> there's gonna be some walking done.[21]
> (Traditional)
> Well now it's two, there's two trains running
> Well ain't nary one (ho)—going my way.[22]
> —Muddy Waters

In *Two Trains Running*, Wilson's construction of "whiteness" reveals the continuing hegemony of the white man. Caught in the vicious cycle of poverty, unemployment, policing, and violence, the denizens of Memphis's diner anecdotally reveal the "status quo" of continued "nigger stacking." Inevitably, all the money ends up in the white man's hands.

> That's all you got around here is niggers with somebody else's money in their pocket. And they don't do nothing but trade it off on each other. I got it today and you got it tomorrow. Until sooner or later, as sure as the sun shine...somebody gonna take it and give it to the white man. The money go from you to me to you and

---

21   August Wilson, *Two Trains Running*, preface.

22   McKinley "Muddy Waters" Morganfield, "Still a Fool" (1951), as quoted in Shannon, *The Dramatic Vision of August Wilson*, 171.

then—bingo, it's gone. You give it to the white man. Pay your rent, pay your telephone, buy your groceries, see the doctor—Bingo, it's gone.... (33–34)

Even the intruder Sterling, another of Wilson's "warrior spirits," comes to the ghetto from a stint in the penitentiary, incarcerated for naïvely trying to take money from the place where wealthy Mellon had stashed it, the bank. Hence, the lesson for 1969, as in Hellman's dramas of the Thirties and Forties, exposes the great economic disparity between the "haves" (whites) and "have nots" (blacks) in America. Memphis provides the only success story as the one black person who's gone into a business for himself who does not rely on death or illegal activity or the government dole. The others who've remained in a section of the city slated for demolition have eked out a living by running numbers (Wolf), operating a funeral parlor (West), living on social security (Holloway) or welfare (Hambone) or working as a waitress for Memphis (Risa). Getting from day to day is the main occupation here. Consequently, money takes on more importance than humanity itself.

In regard to the construction of whiteness in *Two Trains Running*, several generalizations can be made. The white man has most of the money. He owns most of the property in the ghetto and plans to sell it to the city at a healthy profit. In the meantime, he's pulled out the supermarket, the two drugstores, the five-and-ten, doctor and dental offices. Even Zanelli hasn't fixed the jukebox for the last year. Construction and junkyards that pay blacks less than they need to live on still exist. All that's left behind is the undertaker West and "niggers killing one another" (9). The poverty is so frustrating that Risa's brother Rodney moves to Cleveland "before he kill somebody" (18). Even Sterling says: "If I can't find no job I might have to find me a gun" (53). Prophet Samuel survives through his alliance with Mellon and his banking services plus police protection and religion. Ironically Prophet Samuel becomes the very symbol of economic prosperity thought to belong only to whites. So powerful a figure that West even hires Mason, a former cop with a history of shooting blacks, to keep blacks from robbing money and jewelry off Prophet Samuel's body! Whites, the Alberts, even rig the numbers so that the black man can't make too much money. The police photograph black folks at the Malcolm X rally. Half the time the government cheats workers out of their income tax returns. So, while slavery is supposedly over, economic oppression continues with support from whites in the banks and moneylenders, the city government, the police and the prisons, the legal system, and some blacks like Bean, who overcharges his brothers for gas, or West, who tries to get Memphis's property for less than it's worth. In this play, whiteness and economics go hand in hand. Holloway puts the situation this way: "the people out there trying to figure out how they gonna eat. It's day off on the plantation. They waiting for the white man to call them back to work" (104). Independence for the black man lies in the development of his own work, not in the slavery-old reliance on the white man to give it to him.

For Wilson, survival and success depend upon the realization of self-worth and an understanding of the rules by which white men operate. While desperation for money and the loss of a foster parent impelled the orphan Sterling to bank robbery, the new ex-con is the character who hears both the "black is beautiful" message of Black Power and grabs Lutz's ham as tribute to Hambone's worth. Aunt Ester (ancestor) teaches Sterling how to "wash his soul clean" and to be "right with himself," unlike Prophet Samuel who pursues the white man for money (22). Memphis cuts through all the talk with his acute perception that Hambone's failure to get the ham for painting the fences lay precisely in his relinquishment of authority to the white man to determine the value of his work.

> That ain't how it went. Lutz told him if he painted his fence he'd give him a chicken. Told him if he do a good job he'd give him a ham. He think he did a good job and Lutz didn't. That where he went wrong—lettin' Lutz decide what to pay him for his work. If you leave it like that, quite naturally he gonna say it ain't worth the higher price. (23)

Importantly, Memphis fires black attorney Chauncy Ward III, son of a black judge who was "death on niggers," because he wouldn't fight for Memphis's property rights against the white bureaucracy of the city of Pittsburgh. Memphis refuses to hang onto that "old backward southern mentality" wherein "these niggers" tip their hats and jump off the sidewalk for the white Captain/Major (30). Consequently, Memphis hires a white lawyer who enables him to sell his property for what it's worth as well. Memphis understands that when it comes to the city buying and selling property:

> They give white folks a good price. Most time that be who they buying it from. Well, they gonna give me just like they give them. I bought it eight years ago for fifty-five hundred dollars and I ain't taking a penny less than twenty-five thousand. (10)

The big surprise lies in that fact that the white lawyer gets more money for the property than Memphis had imagined! What is significant here is not simply the cash, but what property ownership and a real job mean to Memphis.

> I had seen a way for me to take off my pistol. I got my deed and went right home...took off my pistol and hunt it up in the closet. West got mad when he found out L.D. sold me the building. He been trying to buy it from me ever since. He

walked in the next day and offered me eight thousand dollars for it. That was a good price. But see...he didn't know it had come to mean more to me than that. I had found a way to live the rest of my life. (9)

He doesn't need to accumulate land for itself the way Hartzberger (white) and West (black) do, for what good is it to be land poor and still live over a funeral parlor? As in other Wilson plays, the acquisition of property or land is important only if it guarantees a modicum of independence as it did to the founding fathers. Memphis finds the inner strength to conquer his fear of whiteness and intends to reclaim his land in Jackson, Mississippi from Stovall. This is the same man who had castrated his mule, burned his crops and garnered a white judge's disqualification of the deed of sale because Memphis had located water on the land. Memphis even thinks of setting up a new restaurant on Centre Street where he can provide more jobs for black folks, the kind of community-building Wilson sees as necessary to African American survival and advancement.

Set in 1948, *Seven Guitars* opens its first flashback with its main character, blues singer Floyd Barton, a recently returned war veteran flush with victory, hot on the female trail, and dancing to his own current hit record "That's All Right" on the radio. Despite this optimistic mood, the $47.00 adjustment allowance from the government in Floyd's pocket presages the play's destination. We already know in the first scene that Floyd has been murdered, but the tragedy lies in the later revelation that he's been slaughtered by one of his own, King Hedley. Floyd's speech to Vera reveals the reason for the killing:

> I got to go back. The record company up there waiting on me. They don' sent me a letter telling me to come on back. I wanna go back and take you with me. I ain't gonna be here long. I just got to get my guitar out the pawnshop. I might have to pawn my thirty-eight. You still got my thirty-eight, don' you?... I sat down there doing them ninety days, I told myself it's a good thing I didn't have that with me when they arrested me. Talking about vagrancy.... If I had that thirty-eight they would have tried to dig a hole and put me under the jail. As it was, they took me down there and charged me with worthlessness. Canewell had five dollars in his pocket and they let him go. Took me down there and give me ninety days....[23]

After the guard charges him with threatening to burn the jail down, the judge gives Floyd ninety days for *worthlessness*, and says: "Rockefeller worth a million dollars and you ain't worth two cents" (9). Floyd Barton has to return to Chicago where "You get you a hit record and the white folks call you Mister. Mister Floyd Barton" (10). Floyd equates success with money.

---

[23] August Wilson, *Seven Guitars*, 9.

Despite the white government's improvements in health care for blacks (Hedley can now go to the sanitarium and doesn't need to die from TB) and public adulation for the Brown Bomber's boxing prowess, the white message for the black man is an ambiguous one, to say the least.

> FLOYD: Now here's what I don't understand. If I go out there and punch a white man in the mouth, they give me five years even if there ain't no witnesses. Joe Louis beat up a white man in front of a hundred thousand people and they give him a million dollars. Now you explain that to me.
> RED CARTER: He got a license and you don't. He's registered with the government and you ain't. (58)

White economic exploitation and policing of the Negro continues whether it takes the form of T.L. Hall's fraudulent insurance scheme or management of Floyd's musical career which "turns big money into small" (79) or the record company's refusal to pay Canewell the agreed-upon price. Without the paperwork authorizing Floyd's thirty cents a day earned at the workhouse, Floyd can't even redeem his guitar from the pawnshop. The police pick up Canewell for "disturbing the peace, soliciting without a license, or loitering" (23) in Chicago and even shoot Mrs. Tillery's boy Poochie in the back for robbing the loan offices of Metro Finance (98) while Floyd escapes with the money.

Hedley is right when he says "the white man got a plan" (71) to sabotage the leadership potential in Floyd. Unfortunately, Floyd limits the American notion of equal opportunity to the accumulation of material goods.

> Chicago is what you make it.... It got whatever you want. That's why everybody go there. That's why I'm going there. I'm going there to take advantage of the opportunity.... I'm gonna put out some more records. I know what will make a hit record. I leave here on the Greyhound and I bet you in one year's time I be back driving a Buick. Might even have a Cadillac. If you come visit me you be able to use my telephone. I'm gonna have everything. Some nice furniture. The white man ain't the only one can have a car and nice furniture. Nice clothes. It takes a fool to sit around and don't want nothing. I ain't no fool. It's out there for somebody it may as well be out there for me. (80)

Unfortunately, Floyd does not hear Canewell, who tells Floyd he doesn't want to return to Chicago because the white man treated him like a dog: "it wasn't all about the money. He treat me like he didn't care nothing about me." Instead Floyd subscribes to the notion that the white man "don't have to care nothing about you. You all doing business. He ain't got to like you. Tell him, Red, you got to take advantage of the opportunity while its there" (47). When Floyd takes from Canewell the stolen money that resulted in Poochie's death, Hedley retaliates against Floyd's choice of "opportunity" over his black brother's life.

August Wilson in *Seven Guitars* turns his focus away from the continuing economic oppression of blacks by whites to the real psychological source of continued poverty and violence—the lack of self-esteem within the black man and the equation of success with money. Wilson comes full circle from his exposure of the co-optation of black culture in Levee's attempt to gain white approval by altering Ma's music in *Ma Rainey's Black Bottom* to Floyd's similar attempt in *Seven Guitars*. The black man dies as a result. Neither aping the white man's lifestyle on the plantation like King Hedley or using his .38 like Floyd will lead the black man to genuine independence if he does not possess the pride in race and ancestry personified by King Hedley. Floyd Barton may be "King of the Jungle," but he's lost his focus in "searching out the new land." Economic repression certainly limits individual freedom, but the division and betrayal within the black community it feeds simply recreates those very conditions white folks left behind in the Old World—poverty, prison, social ostracism, and death.

Lillian Hellman and August Wilson examine the black/white interface to expose the evolving and expanding nature of an American identity. Both share a value system embraced by the Constitution and the Bill of Rights and expose the economic inequities that serve to repress freedom in America. Hellman's dramas, largely written during the Thirties and Forties long before the Civil Rights Movement, present black characters who occupy service positions in white households, yet she imbues Addie, Coralee, Sophronia and Henry with enormous moral stature and influence upon those very white people for whom they work. Hellman shares a belief in economic justice and a strong work ethic with August Wilson and repudiates the treatment of the black man, or any person for that matter, as property. Wilson's white characters attach themselves to black men primarily to make money off them. He attempts to reposition the black man in American society by bolstering his sense of worth as a human being to counteract slavery's psychological damage and an ongoing state of economic repression by the white hegemony. For both authors, fairness, however difficult and awkward between black and white, is all.

CHAPTER THREE

Lillian Hellman: Rewriting History

Hellman writes domestic family drama to create a place where issues of responsibility and political dynamics are worked out. Hellman mines her family memories and life's experiences here and in Europe to combat a kind of national forgetfulness and self-interested isolation.[1] History-making goes beyond a documented sequence of events into a quest for identity. Set largely in family living rooms with attached terraces or gardens, Hellman's plays only rarely move to other sites—hotel rooms, a girls' school or offices. Even the most affluent and insulated wealthy Americans are subject to invasion within the walls of their own homes where memory and history intersect.

The Children's Hour

Hellman's settings are specific sites housing a theatrical event in which a dramatic turning point ruptures the very fabric of society. In her first play *The Children's Hour*, she moves an actual 19th-century Scottish legal case involving the ruin of two teachers by a false accusation of lesbianism to a New England girls' school. The Massachusetts site of the Dobie-Wright School takes the audience to the very seat of the American Revolution, the home of America's "founding fathers." The play's opening gives us a deceptive glimpse of normal, everyday goings-on in the girls' school, a social organism through which Hellman begins her dramatic examination of the values of the society in which we live, the mores taught to the young through our educational system. It may be apocryphal that George Washington could not tell a lie, but certainly for Hellman a lie was "an annihilation of dignity";[2] stealing, "the moral invasion of other people's rights."[3]

The literary quotations the students recite testify to Hellman's early concern with social justice. She applies Alexander Pope's maxim "The proper study of mankind is man," who in turn is the "Sole judge of truth, in endless error hurl'd/ The glory, jest, and riddle of the world!"[4] While Hellman takes

---

1   Lillian Hellman, "Bethe," *Pentimento*, 309–53.
2   Lillian Hellman, *Pentimento*, 299.
3   Lillian Hellman, *Unfinished Woman*, 303.
4   Alexander Pope, *The Essay On Man*, Epistle 2, Lines 2, 17–18.

humorous advantage of Catherine's "How much longer, O Catiline, are you going to abuse our patience?,"[5] she is textually setting up the rupturing event. A child's lie accusing two teachers of lesbianism—fueled by the very human need for attention and a resistance to authority—leads to the development of a conspiracy against those in power and forecasts a future court trial. All this out of the use of Cicero's prosecution of Catiline for his intended revolt against the Roman government! The specific subject of the play will indeed become a dissection of how "One master passion in the breast, like Aaron's serpent, swallows all the rest"—the use and abuse of power.[6]

Unlike her other plays, Hellman bases *The Children's Hour* on a real-life court case. Dashiell Hammett suggested that she read the actual trial narrative from 1810 contained in "Closed Doors; or The Great Drumsheugh Case," one of a collection of criminal cases entitled *Bad Companions* by William Roughead.[7] While Hellman retains many plot elements and personae contained in the court narrative in addition to the failure to disprove the claim of lesbianism by exposing the lie, she makes several very interesting changes. Hellman's Mary Tilford is a young, spoiled, wealthy little girl drawn from Hellman's own experience who effectively hides her wish not to go to school by manipulating her elders and bullying her peers. From her own life, Hellman was familiar with the exciting prospect of acquiring adult knowledge,[8] eavesdropping,[9] "the powers of an only child,"[10] "a child's malice,"[11] and a precocious desire for independence.[12] Describing her exaltation in running away from home and hiding out at the black boardinghouse in *An Unfinished Woman*, she wrote: "I knew my power over my parents."[13] In the play, parents and grandmother—adults filled with a romantic belief in the innocence of children and a parental wish to protect their offspring from a possible threat of lesbianism—fail to perceive the truth behind Mary's attempt to destroy her teachers through character assassination.

Hellman alters documented history to explore hate crime and its abuse of freedom. Hellman's character is completely different from her real-life model Jane Cumming, the half-black illegitimate child of Lady Cumming

5　　Cicero, *Orations*. Quoted in *The Children's Hour*, *The Collected Plays* (Boston: Little, Brown & Co., 1972), 9.
6　　Pope, *Essay On Man*, Epistle 2, Lines 131–32.
7　　William Roughead, *Bad Companions* (New York: Duffield and Green, 1931).
8　　Lillian Hellman, *Pentimento*, 331.
9　　*Ibid.*, 335.
10　Lillian Hellman, *An Unfinished Woman*, 18.
11　*Ibid.*
12　*Ibid.*, 35, 22.
13　*Ibid.*, 39.

Gordon's son from India. Hellman eliminated racial comments contained in the court proceedings, referring to her as "half caste" or "black sheep,"[14] to focus on the child's abuse of power by bringing up the then-taboo notion of lesbianism. In fact, Jane Cumming visited her grandmother legally and did not run away like Hellman or Mary.

Hellman also adapts the historical model for Mrs. Mortar, a Mrs. Woods who was an ex-Shakespearean actress known for her presentation of *The Mourning Bride*.[15] Hellman chooses to give her Portia's speech from the *Merchant of Venice* and also makes Mrs. Mortar Martha's aunt (the original Mrs. Woods was the aunt of the model for Karen). Nor was there ever a Joe Cardin. Hellman uses these last two changes to distinguish between the two teachers. Karen has a heterosexual relationship while Martha discovers the possibility of her feelings for Karen and ultimately commits suicide. Another major change occurs in the use of Mrs. Tilford. Hellman suggests a course of action to remedy the situation. Her character returns to the school and attempts to help the young teachers after she learns of Mary's lie. In real life, Lady Cumming Gordon continued to persecute the two teachers even after they had won an appeal. Both lived separately with friends, but never regained their careers. This major alteration allows Karen, Martha and Joe, a relative of Mary's grandmother, the wealthy and socially powerful Mrs. Tilford, to invade her well-appointed parlor to plead their case. In the new setting—a metaphor for power and status—the two young women, who have worked for eight years during the Depression to build their school, don't stand a chance. Only with the revelation of Mary's blackmailing of Rosalie with the stolen bracelet does Mrs. Tilford relent, but too late to prevent Martha's suicide. Hence, a child's manipulation of a lie containing a social/sexual taboo wreaks havoc on the school and its teachers and forces the public to question whether the proceedings and mores of society are indeed just. Hellman's early use of the Portia speech now makes sense:

> "It is twice blest; it blesseth him that gives and him that takes: 'tis mightiest in the mightiest; it becomes the throned monarch better than his crown; his sceptre shows the force of temporal power, the attribute to awe and majesty, wherein..." doth sit the dread and fear of kings; but mercy is above this sceptred sway, it is enthroned in the hearts of kings, it is an attribute to God himself; and earthly power doth then show likest God's when mercy seasons justice." We do pray for mercy, and that same prayer doth teach....[16]

---

14 Roughead, 120.
15 *Ibid.,* 118.
16 William Shakespeare, *The Merchant of Venice.* Quoted in *The Children's Hour,* 7–8.

Thus the audience learns to value the importance of "innocent until proven guilty" and the necessity of responsible action within the American system.

Days to Come

The Children's Hour refers to the Depression only by remarking the cost of a telephone call or a taxi and the eight years necessary for Karen and Martha to build the school. *Days to Come*, Hellman's 1936 drama reflecting the vogue of strike/labor plays constituting more than a fifth of the 1935–1936 Broadway season,[17] tackles the difficult economics of labor's struggle for survival more directly. The arrival of strikebreakers to deal with unrest at a midwestern brush factory signals the dangerous moment of change that will eventually culminate in confrontation between strikers and scabs. The leading strikebreaker Easter kills his henchman Mossie onstage to frame the labor organizer Whalen and provide an excuse for violent attacks on the strikers. His murder of the strike leader Firth's child effectively ends the strike, the possibility of a living wage, and an old-fashioned community-based loyalty between employer and employees. In *Days to Come*, wealth and criminality unite to prevent the economic rise of desperate factory workers.

Hellman sites the play in one of her characteristic well-appointed drawing rooms of the wealthy, here the owners of a brush factory significantly located in America's capitalistic heartland, the manufacturing Midwest. The Rodman house is located in Callom, Ohio about two hundred miles from Cleveland. The room is designed to impress outsiders with "all furniture giving the impression of being arranged for the entrance doors."[18] The circular porch is the entrance used "by people who know the house well" (81). Hellman describes the overall effect: "the room is beautiful, simple. But the objects in the cabinet are too neatly placed and the effect is rigid and bad" (81). The precise placement of objects in the room reflects the rigid class-conscious personality of the sister of factory owner Andrew Rodman, Cora. She clings to her securities and condemns the immorality of a local, poor thirteen-year-old girl pregnant with an illegitimate child. Cora also criticizes her "careless" sister-in-law Julie, the first to enter from the porch, for forgetting the tree planting. Julia's response testifies to the family's unwillingness to adapt to difficult socioeconomic conditions and the consequent awkwardness of the worker families toward the Rodmans.

---

[17] Doris V. Falk, *Lillian Hellman* (New York: Frederick Ungar Publishing Co., 1978), 46–47.

[18] Lillian Hellman, *Days to Come*, 81.

CORA: You know my rules. Not to interfere.
JULIE: There are so many rules. It's hard to remember them all. It's funny to go walking now. The Carsen kids were coming from school. They had a bad minute wondering whether to say hello to me. (87)

Hellman establishes the conflict between the haves and have-nots, between traditional employer/employee loyalty and the economic necessity for fair wages, by placing Cora's self-interested tight-fistedness in direct contrast to the generosity of the household help. Hannah and the servant girl, loyal to the Rodman family for twenty years, give money out of their meager wages and food to the strikers and Hannah's sister provides lodging for the strike organizer Whalen.

Hellman refuses to allow the Rodman living room to remain sacrosanct. Instead, she invades their sanctuary from within and without with the arrival of Henry Ellicott, Andrew Rodman's business partner, lawyer and his wife's lover, as well as strikers, labor organizer and gangster scabs. Ellicott does business from the Rodman living room and exerts control over Andrew Rodman when he orders the deployment of hired strikebreakers and overrides, with Cora's support, Andrew's objections to this decision. Ellicott controls the Rodman marriage both in his affair with Julie and his joint surveillance (along with Cora) of Julie's activities, including her walks near the strike office.

The major external invasion occurs as Firth, longtime Rodman employee, and Whalen the labor organizer, enter *from the porch* on the heels of Ellicott's warning Julie "not to start anything" (90). Firth brings Whalen, who's received a telegram naming the strikebreakers, to protest the use of scabs who are no more than "foreigners" and "hired guns." The arrival of scab boss Wilkie and his thugs Easter and Mossie puts an end to Firth's objections and they take over the living room to "protect" the Rodman family. Act I ends with the titillating double threat of sex and violence giving the lie to the "society picture" of the Rodmans who "They say, in the papers, talking fine, what they wouldn't do, and then they sneak off and take a shot in bed at the first thing that comes along" (101).

In just a few pages, Hellman exposes the class conflict she sees in the larger capitalistic society and demarcates sides in the ensuing struggle. She adds emotional complexity through the shared friendship and loyalty between Firth and Andrew Rodman and the implied love interest between Julie and Whalen. When even the servants refuse to open the door to the strikebreakers, we in the audience know that we're sitting in on the cusp of change, the state of emergency where the *status quo* is under attack. The moment of danger affects the content of tradition and its receivers. Pursuit of profit will destroy the town's traditional loyalty between employer and employees.

Act II opens a month later and shows the gangsters using the Rodman living room as a "club," smoking, playing cards, and listening to the radio. In a fight over gambling debts, Easter murders Mossie (in the living room) and Wilkie decides to frame Whalen by planting the body near his office. Hellman thus introduces the first murder into the very stronghold of the wealthy, the seat of power, and anticipates the violence soon to erupt outside. Wilkie's boys, soon sworn in as deputy sheriffs, can now label the strikers "un-American"! A peculiar, self-interested interpretation of the Puritan work ethic put in service to a perversion of the justice system, equal opportunity, and free speech!

In true cinematic and metaphorical fashion, Hellman then moves "outside" to Whalen's "bare and clean" office to give the audience a sense of what is happening with the "have-nots," the factory workers. This bare bones workplace accentuates Whalen's idealism and contrasts with the luxurious Rodman setting. The audience finds out that Whalen is an unselfish and practiced idealist dedicated to helping the laborers, that the workers' children aren't getting enough food and the thugs have been hassling Firth's adopted child to frighten him. In this scene, we get to know the real Whalen, a gardener's son who went to college for a few months, hoboed and developed a hatred for the denigration, meanness, and cowardice that come with poverty. Tough-talking, pragmatic, and idealistic, Whalen's persona attracts Julie.

> When I was young, I guess I was looking for something I could do. Then for something I could be.... Finally, just for something to want, or to think, or to believe in. I always wanted somebody to show me the way. (108)

Julie's naïve purposelessness, a warning to those who act without values in American society, endangers Whelan and accentuates her wealthy negligence. He, however, will have nothing to do with the boss's wife and gets her out of the office. The cinematic scene ends with Whalen drinking and smoking, ignorant of Mosse's corpse outside and waiting for the sheriff's knock. Scene II moves back to the Rodman household where Wilkie, significantly now in the darkened living room, stands facing the front door. He and Ellicott conspire to subvert justice by getting Judge Alcott to ignore the impending violence and allow them to arrest Whelan for murder. Once Whelan is out of the way, the strikebreakers can provoke the workers into a fight. Andrew attempts to stop the promised attack on his townspeople in their own homes, but Ellicott and Wilkie overrule him as gunfire breaks out. The new, corrupt union of high society people, law enforcers, and common criminals is complete.

The final act depicts the results. No longer will the old sense of allegiance to each other in the town community be the same. Julie questions Andrew's permitting the violence and reveals Whalen's innocence of the crime. Consequently, Andrew calls the judge. However, as often happens with Hellman's well-intended, "innocent" wealthy, Rodman's actions come too late. Firth arrives to call off the strike because his daughter has been murdered. Rodman loses both his town and himself as a result.

> Last night I lost the place and the land where I was born. I can't go downtown, he said. It isn't safe. It isn't safe for me to go into that town. You see what I mean. I lost what I thought I was. I lost Firth his child. (128)

Hellman's play is not, however, just the story of one man. It is an indictment of a socioeconomic system in which the wealthy buy off the judges and the police in a class struggle that is a travesty of the notion of American democracy. Whalen puts it this way to Firth, who is distraught because he and Andrew Rodman can no longer be good friends.

> WHALEN: I know. And you're as good as he is. It says so in the book. Until the time comes. Look. You're on one side. He's on the other. That's lesson number one. Don't let'em tell you that because your grandfather voted for Jefferson you're any different from some Polack in Pittsburgh whose grandfather couldn't write his name. You're on the same side the Polack is, and that's where you belong.
> FIRTH: Well, maybe we'll try again some day.
> WHALEN: I hope so. And the guy they send in my place, you give him a better chance. (128)

Wilkie collects his money from Andrew, who refuses to shake his hand, and points out the essential hypocrisy of the situation in which a well-meaning manager leaves a legacy of destruction.

> I've worked for a lot of men, some of them deacons of the church who were breaking strikes for the good of America, but I never worked for a man before who believed I could come in, run his factory, and break his strike without walking on anybody's toes.... (123–24)

Andrew's sharp retort to Ellicott's comment that "We've been fighting your husband's battles for him" leads Andrew to admit his complicity:

> That's quite true. The delicate prince in his ivory tower—was carefully protected from the dust and din of battle. You are noble warriors and you've done a noble night's work. I'll see to it that when the history is written, it won't be mentioned that you were fighting for yourself, too. (124)

While sardonically put, Andrew's comment speaks to the notion of history as a story told by those in power. After all, Andrew Rodman may have lost his town and disenchanted his "careless" wife, but Ellicott remains in charge and leaves for Silver Springs. Cora, drinking milk "as if she needed it," pretends that nothing ever happened (123–25). In *Pentimento*, Hellman rightly summed up *Days to Come* in the following fashion:

> It is crowded and overwrought, but it is a good report of rich liberals in the 1930s, of a labor leader who saw through them, of a modern lost lady, and has in it a correct prediction of how conservative the American labor movement was to become. (465)

The Little Foxes and Another Part of the Forest

Unlike *The Children's Hour* and *Days to Come*, Hellman moves her settings to the deep South in the two plays which bookend World War II, *The Little Foxes* and *Another Part of the Forest*. In *Unfinished Woman*, she describes the difficulties inherent in trying to craft a play from her own life. After struggling through nine drafts of *The Little Foxes*, she wrote:

> Some of the trouble came because the play has a distant connection to my mother's family and everything that I had heard or seen or imagined had formed a giant tangled time-jungle in which I could find no space to walk without tripping over old roots, hearing old voices speak about histories made long before my day. (424)

In *Pentimento* she writes:

> My father turned to me. "Your mother's family are not killers of white people. Remember that and be proud. They never do more than beat up niggers who can't pay fifty percent interest on the cotton crop and that's how they got rich." (336)

Hellman may have "watched my mother's family increase their fortune on the borrowings of poor Negroes," but her sense of history reaches far beyond the personal to a consideration of the evolution of American history itself. She considers the American Civil War as a major turning point that destroys much of what went before it, an ante-bellum South based on an agrarian economic system upholding the planters at the top, slaves on the bottom, and merchants in-between. The latter's rise to wealth and power at the expense of the Southern aristocracy and the cheap labor of former slaves finds its expression in characters based on Hellman family members and the environments which house them. Her settings metaphorically illustrate her fascination for the use and abuse of power as observed at family dinners and the "injustice of socially ordained inferiority visited especially on blacks and on women."[19] In the two dramas, she plays with personal and national "histories made long before my day."

Another Part of the Forest (1946), while composed ostensibly to give us the background of characters met earlier in *The Little Foxes*, positions the Hubbards, newly wealthy from profits made during the Civil War and Reconstruction, ascending to a position of power and privilege despite opposition from the old Southern society. The year (1880) is one of transition and great change; the place a veritable battlefield as in Shakespeare's *Titus Andronicus*. "Another part of the forest" in the bard's war-torn Roman Empire is "ruthless, dreadful, deaf, and dull."[20] It's the place where Tamora's sons rape Lavinia, chaste daughter of Titus, and murder the new emperor Bassanius. Hellman appropriately applies the name of Titus' tribune brother, Marcus, to the head of the Hubbard family. Interestingly enough, Webster's *New Collegiate Dictionary* points to "marchier" as the root word meaning "to trample" (Fr) and the noun (marc) as "the residue remaining after a fruit has been pressed."[21] There is a definite connection between the earlier generation of Hubbards, led by Marcus, and his offspring who fox-like rape the vineyard, the South of *The Little Foxes*. A blockade runner who sold salt at exorbitant prices, Marcus ruthlessly trampled on the Confederate world to make money and led Union men to the Confederate camp where 27 young soldiers were massacred. Hated by the old gentry as represented by Colonel Isham who reports Oscar's Ku Klux Klan activity, Marcus now aspires to the social position held by the ante-bellum gentry. He forces Isham to drink coffee with him, lavishly pays off the old veteran and thereby arouses hatred and a desire for revenge in his own sons who must repay Marcus. His repressive rule over his own family will cause Ben's takeover and Marcus' dethronement.

The play itself and its setting become a site for a series of invasions. First Marcus Hubbard infiltrated "enemy" lines to profit from the need for salt and led Union troops to the Confederate camp. Later he invaded the center of this old Southern town of Bowden, Alabama and moved into the Reed House bought after the Civil War. The two-story Greek Revival house has a porch above, a portico leading into the living room, and a view of the main street across a front lawn. Hellman links the architecture with the Greek golden age and the action with the decline of the Roman Empire. Consequently she invites the audience to compare American history with that of Greece and Rome. Hellman describes the set in the following fashion:

---

19   Richard Poirier, introduction to Lillian Hellman, *Three: An Unfinished Woman, Pentimento, Scoundrel Time* (Boston & Toronto: Little, Brown & Co., 1979), xvi.

20   *Titus Andronicus*, II, i, 128.

21   *Webster's New Collegiate Dictionary* (Springfield, MA: G&C Merriam Co., 1977), 702.

> The main part of the house, built in the 1850s is Southern Greek. It is not a great
> mansion but it is a good house built by a man of taste from whom Marcus Hubbard
> bought it after the Civil War. There is not much furniture on the portico: two chairs
> and a table at one end, one comfortable chair and a table at the other end. Twin
> heads of Aristotle are on high pedestals. There is something too austere, too pre-
> tended Greek about the portico, as if it followed one man's eccentric taste and was
> not designed to be comfortable for anyone else.[22]

Classical Greek pretensions abound in both the architecture with its later col-
onnade additions and in the furnishings which include busts of Aristotle, a
glass-enclosed Greek vase on a pedestal, a Greek statue, and paintings of
Greek battle scenes. Hellman makes it clear that the furniture is from the
previous owner and that there is a severity to the living room not common to
many rooms of the 1880s. This is an invaded house, not a home: the recently
acquired site of the "nouveau riche"—the spoils of war.

Marcus operates like a Greek tyrant/king who has seized the house as
war booty, keeps his sons on a tight financial rope as employees, spoils a
luxury-loving daughter whose sexuality is a tool unlike the Shakespearean
Lavinia's chastity, disregards his wife Lavinia's religiosity and care for black
folk, and suggests to Ben that he read a little Aristotle to take his mind off
money (348). Just as the Romans took over from the Greeks, so too does
Marcus the merchant—aspiring to aristocratic culture and status—adopt the
accoutrements of culture (classical learning and music) to become like the
Southern aristocracy he has displaced.

> At nine years old I was carrying water for two bits a week. I took the first dollar I
> ever had and went to the paying library to buy a card. When I was twelve I was
> working out in the fields, and that same year I taught myself Latin and French. At
> fourteen I was driving mules all day and most of the night, but that was the year I
> learned my Greek, read my classics, taught myself—Think what I must have wanted
> for sons. And then think what I got. One unsuccessful trickster, one proud illiterate.
> No, I don't think Oscar's ever read a book. (348)

Marcus gloats over the notion of the "Bagtrys in this house, begging" (330).
To solve the Bagtry financial troubles, Birdie has to swallow her pride to sell
paintings and silver to the very people her mother would never acknowledge.
Birdie knows, as Regina points out, that Marcus "could buy and sell Lionnet
on the same morning, its cotton and its women with it."

Another Part of the Forest employs two sets: the side portico (Acts I &
III) and the living room (Act II). Clearly the portico contextualizes the town
and the larger Southern society whereas the living room takes us inside the
family itself. Act I presents Bowden's invaders; Act II shows the invaders

---

[22]   Lillian Hellman, *Another Part of the Forest*, 329.

invaded by fading aristocrats, hired musicians, and even a hooker; Act III introduces the second generation who will become the powerful and ruthless industrialists of the future pictured in *The Little Foxes*.

Hellman opens the play with a picture straight out of a Harlequin romance or *Gone with the Wind* — an aristocratic John Bagtry, dressed in shabby riding shirt and Confederate Cavalry pants, addressing a young and beautiful woman in déshabillé, nightgown and negligée. John Bagtry is a living *lieu de mémoire* in his fifteen-year-old Confederate uniform, a visual residue of history, a man trapped in the past. Hellman will repeat and render indelible the image of the unadaptable aristocrat in Oscar's final depiction (390) of Bagtry dressed like Robert E. Lee leaving town to join Cod Carter defending the plantation way of life in Brazil. Like her father, Regina envies the "breeding" and social status John Bagtry represents and hopes to join Southern "high society" through marriage. Bagtry's concern with other people seeing them and potential scandal, however, is minor compared to the notion that he was "only good once — in a war" (331, 366) and must join another one in Brazil defending planters and slavery.

Friction within mirrors the friction outside. Because Marcus rules the household with an iron hand, Regina, Ben and Oscar compete for position and money among themselves in order to get what they want. Once Ben grasps control over the Hubbard fortune, he tells his father:

> Now you take you, Papa. You were smart in your day and figured out what fools you lived among. But ever since the war you been too busy getting cultured, or getting Southern. A few more years and you'd have been just like the rest of them. (402)

His sons Ben and Oscar, interested in money and whores respectively, could not care less about education or culture.

Act I presents the now wealthy Hubbards occupying the center in a poorer and largely resentful town context. At the play's beginning, Lavinia Hubbard returns to the mansion with her black servant Coralee from the Christian "nigger" church. Significantly, her empathy with black folk sets her apart from the Hubbards within the house. Next a former war hero, Colonel Isham, demands compensation for Oscar's participation in a Ku Klux Klan attack on "carpetbagger" Taylor and mentions how everyone in the county would be pleased to "swing up anybody called Hubbard" (316) who engages in a "personal war on the people of this state" (315). Ben does not mince words about the volatility of the environment that Oscar's gun-toting could ignite:

> Now listen to me, you clown. You put away your gun and keep it away. If those
> fools in your Klan want to beat up niggers and carpetbaggers, you let 'em do it. But
> you're not going to make this country dangerous to me, or dangerous to the busi-
> ness. We had a hard enough time making them forget Papa made too much money
> out of the war, and I ain't ever been sure they forgot it. (342)

Oscar, angered by his father's financial domination, takes out his frustration
on blacks and Northerners and takes up with the local whore Laurette. He
defies Ben who had bought his way out of fighting in the Civil War:

> Course they haven't forgot it. Every time anybody has two drinks, or you call up an-
> other loan, there's plenty of talk, and plenty of hints I don't understand. *(Rises.)* If I
> had been old enough to fight in the war, you just bet I'd been right there, and not
> like you, bought off. I'm a Southerner. And when I see an old carpetbagger or up-
> start nigger, why, I feel like taking revenge. (343)

Here Hellman has extrapolated beyond a single individual to the exposure of
a whole set of white trash attitudes about what values make up the post-war
American South: excluding "foreigners," i.e. Northerners, keeping African
Americans down, and taking over those privileges once possessed by the aristocracy alone.

Act II moves inside the living room for the "musicale" to which the
"quality folk" (Birdie and John Bagtry) and Oscar's whore Laurette have
been invited. Lavinia lets us know that these are the first guests "since the
suspicion on your Papa," hinting at some well-hidden family secret. The oc-
casion gives Marcus the opportunity to show off his newly-acquired culture
by playing solo violin in his own composition. However, Laurette blows
apart his and Oscar's pretensions. To her, the Hubbards are no better than
"piney wood crooks" and she's every bit as good as they are: "Pretend? I'm
as good as anybody called Hubbard. Why, my Pa died at Vicksburg. He
didn't stay home bleeding the whole state of Alabama with money tricks, and
suspected of worse" (361–62).

The big clash, the moment of danger, occurs in the pitting of Marcus versus John Bagtry when John defends his "fight for a way of life" in the Civil
War or in Brazil. Displaying his familiarity with the Greek wars, Marcus
criticizes Bagtry for failing to choose the winning side: "Well, I disapprove
of you. Your people deserved to lose their war and their world. It was a
backward world, getting in the way of history. Appalling that you still don't
realize it. Really, people should read more books" (68) Yet Laurette, the
common whore, is quick to point out the hypocrisy behind Marcus's "pro-
gressive" view of history:

Everybody in this country knows how you got rich, bringing in salt and making poor, dying people give up everything for it. Right in the middle of the war, men dying for you, and you making their kinfolk give you all their goods and money—and I heard how they suspected you of worse, and you only just got out of a hanging rope. *(Points to Oscar.)* Why, the first night he slept with me, I didn't even want to speak to him because of you and your doings. My uncle used to tell me about—. (372)

Marcus kicks the pair out of his house, denies Ben his loan deal to Birdie Bagtry, and refuses to consider a possible marriage of Regina and Bagtry. Yet it is his refusal to allow Lavinia to set up her school for black children at the end of the act that causes the penultimate explosion in Act III.

The living room becomes the battleground for opposing socioeconomic views. Self-interest conflicts with Christian generosity and guilt created by the practice of slavery. The family revolution peaks as Lavinia, determined to leave and have her school, presents another *lieu de mémoire* in the Bible which contains the true account of Marcus's participation in the massacre and his purchase of falsified passes from Captain Virgil E. McMullen. Lavinia provides Ben with the proof he needs to blackmail his father, take over the business, and direct his siblings' lives. After leaving Regina her pin, Oscar her prayer book, Ben her Papa's watch and Marcus her wedding ring, Lavinia takes the Bible and her purse with her. Marcus, now dethroned, gets his cup of coffee but watches Regina signify her new allegiance to Ben as she goes to sit with him at the close of the play.

Harkening back to the roots of Western Civilization in Greek and Roman history, Hellman exposes the decay of spiritual values in the ruthless pursuit of economic advancement. If money can buy everything—including human beings—true culture is lost. Certainly, Marcus's story of self-education is a glorification of the self-made man, the Horatio Alger myth of an America where a better life is open to all. Yet the abuse of his newfound economic power causes his own downfall. Wealth and status generated by the enslaving and cheating of other human beings gives the lie to Christian ethics and the American belief in equal justice and opportunity for all.

Unfortunately, Hellman's depiction of economic exploitation does not terminate with Marcus, but continues on to the next generation. Ben claims the twentieth century as his own.

The century's turning, the world is open. Open for people like you and me. Ready for us, waiting for us. After all this is just the beginning. There are hundreds of Hubbards sitting in rooms like this throughout the country. All their names aren't Hubbard, but they are all Hubbards and they will own this country some day. (197)

Hellman situates *The Little Foxes* in 1900, a pivotal point in history as the South turned from an agrarian to an industrial society. The "moment of danger" in which power and exploitation join hands lies in the deal Southern merchants make with Northern businessmen to become great national industrialists in pursuit of profit. Ben first boasts of the Hubbard takeover of the war-debilitated Southern aristocracy:

> Our grandfather and our father learned the new ways and learned how to make them pay. *(Smiles nastily.)* They were in trade, Hubbard Sons, Merchandise. Others, Birdie's family, for example, looked down on them. To make a long story short, Lionnet now belongs to us. *(Birdie stops playing.)* Twenty years ago we took over their land, their cotton, and their daughter. (158)

Next he invites further invasion from the North in a joint venture bid to construct cotton mills in the South that would still rely on cheap labor (poor whites, blacks, and women) to amass great profits.

Hellman renders judgment on the new giants of industry (the Hubbards and Marshalls of the world) by allowing the black mammy Addie to compare the coming construction of the Hubbard/Marshall cotton mills to the Civil War devastation by William Tecumseh Sherman in his March on Atlanta and Savannah in the winter of 1864. The march destroyed two hundred miles of railroad tracks and resulted in the deaths of thousands of blacks following Sherman's troops.[23] Addie expresses a Southern and humanitarian point of view:

> BIRDIE: Quiet and restful.
> ADDIE: Well, it won't be that way long. Little while now, even sitting here, you'll hear the red bricks going into place. The next day the smoke'll be pushing out the chimneys and by church time that Sunday every human born of woman will be living on chicken. That's how Mr. Ben's been telling the story.
> HORACE: They believe it that way?
> ADDIE: Believe it? They use to believing what Mr. Ben orders. There ain't been so much talk around here since Sherman's army didn't come near.
> HORACE: They are fools.
> ADDIE: You ain't born in the South unless you're a fool. (179)

Hellman warns the audience not to be fools, but to take action. She titles the play, at the suggestion of Dorothy Parker, with a reference to Solomon 2:15: "Take us the foxes, the little foxes that spoil the vines, for our vines have tender grapes."[24] Hellman connected the Hubbards with the foxes who spoil the earth and warns against their continuing legacy in America. She

---

23   Note the appropriateness of Horace's possession of Union Pacific bonds.
24   Doris V. Falk, *Lillian Hellman* (New York: Frederick Ungar Publishing Co.), 51.

tells us not to stand by and let them do it. To Addie, she again gives the voice of judgment:

> Yeah, they got mighty well off cheating niggers. Well, there are people who eat the earth and eat all the people on it like in the Bible with the locusts. Then there are people who stand round and watch them eat it. *(Softly.)* Sometimes I think it ain't right to stand and watch them do it. (182)

The Hubbards' and Marshalls' invasion of the old South finds its *lieu de mémoire* in the set itself where two invasions occur—the South by the North, Regina into the business world. The theatrical space, the site of the deal-making, is an interior one, specifically the living room of the Giddens house in a small town in the South. Within earshot and separated by double doors is the dining room. The play encompasses three weeks in the spring, symbolically the time engendering new growth. The room is good-looking and the furniture expensive; but it reflects "no particular taste." Everything is of the best and that is all. This house is not a "home" in the traditional sense in that there is no idiosyncratic personality influencing the furnishing and reflecting the style of the inhabitants; instead there are only quality goods in the space providing evidence for money as the arbiter of taste and the god in residence. Nor is there any sense that this house is architecturally connected to the antebellum South. Thus, the house signifies America in general.

While she lets business dealings occasionally invade the Rodman living room in *Days to Come*, Hellman also employs the second set of Whalen's office to give us the larger context of the community and world of the not wealthy. In *The Little Foxes*, she upsets the *status quo* by moving the public commercial world completely into the usually private interior of the Giddens house itself. There is no longer any separation between home and workplace. She tightens the focus down to the Giddens living room and moves the public business arena directly into the home, as she had observed it done in her own family. In *Pentimento*, Hellman writes:

> I began to think that greed and the cheating that is its usual companion were comic as well as evil and I began to like the family dinners with the talk of who did what to whom.... I rebelled against my mother's family, and thus all people who were rich, but I was frightened and impressed by them; and the more frightened and impressed I grew the more aimless became my anger which sometimes expressed itself in talk about the rights of Negroes and on two Sundays took the form of deliberately breaking plates at my Grandmother's table. (483; 365–66)

In *The Little Foxes*, Hellman goes beyond her previous plays to present a much enlarged view of history, giving voice to those unheard from before—women and African Americans. Hellman constructs history on several levels: mythological (Bible), national (Ben), regional (South), and familial within the compressed arena of the living room. She centers her drama in the female world of the house interior, emphasizes one major character in Regina Giddens, and introduces the revolutionary notion of a woman becoming a major player in the commercial arena usually reserved to men.

Regina puts it to Birdie: "I said I think you should either be a nigger or a millionaire. In between, like us, what for?"[25] Regina married the wealthy Horace Giddens, advanced by Ben as a suitable wealthy husband of good family in *Another Part of the Forest,* to escape the imprisonment of living at her brother's beck and call. However, she sees no value in being caught in the middle between poverty and wealth. She dislikes the necessity of securing Horace's funds to guarantee partnership in the business deal that would provide her with the freedom and lifestyle in Chicago she craves. So it is in Horace's absence that Regina, according to the black manservant Cal (6), gives the orders to impress Chicago industrialist Marshall, who is celebrating the consummation of a deal bringing the mills to the cotton that will make the Hubbards even richer. For Regina, a share in the business is a consummation more important than sex or family. Consequently, she goads Horace into a heart attack when he obstructs her plan and, in the bone-chilling quiet of her refusal to give him his medicine, virtually murders him. Ultimately, she manipulates her brothers out of 75% of the business through blackmailing them about the theft of the bonds and the subsequent scandal that would effectively terminate the deal.

Regina's newfound financial freedom costs her Zan's love, but enables Hellman to extend the notion of real female emancipation. Hellman trusts Addie, the black mammy, to act as both protector and guide for Regina's daughter, who declares her independence from the Hubbards at the play's end. The strength of the black character as a kind of moral arbiter was so revolutionary that Hellman altered the play for the 1941 film to provide Zan with a boyfriend to free her from life with the Hubbards.

Watch on the Rhine

Working on *Watch on the Rhine* and *The Little Foxes* simultaneously, Hellman did extensive historical research for both plays. She went beyond releasing the individual from an oppressive, exploitative situation in *The Little Foxes* to raising the very question of how an individual can shape or rewrite history on an international scale in *Watch on the Rhine*. While the 1941 Broadway season abounded with war dramas (such as Robert Sherwood's

---

[25]   Lillian Hellman, *The Little Foxes,* 161.

There Shall Be No Night, Philip Barry's *Liberty Jones,* and Maxwell Anderson's *Key Largo* among many others), Hellman's *Watch on the Rhine* was a wake-up call to fascism in Europe and the presence of Nazi sympathizers in America. Winning the New York Drama Critics Circle Award for 1941, the play preceded America's entry into World War II at the bombing of Pearl Harbor and called into question American isolationism. In 1942, the drama was performed in Washington for President Franklin Delano Roosevelt.[26]

In *Watch on the Rhine,* Hellman's work takes on an international perspective based on her study and observation of European events in the Twenties and Thirties coupled with her personal experience of the Spanish Civil War and her literary fascination with Henry James' comparison of Europeans and Americans.[27]

> Only two diaries written at the end of 1938 could convince me now that *Watch on the Rhine* came out of Henry James.... I began to think of James's *The American* and *The Europeans.* In the short time since James the United States had become the dominant country not alone in money and power, but in imposing on other people a morality which was designed in part to hide its self-interest. Was that a new American game or had we learned it from the English who invented it to hold down their lower classes? We still spoke as nineteenth-century Cromwellians in church, home, and university, but increasingly, the more we recognized disorder and corruption at home the more insistent we grew about national purity.
>
> Many Europeans had moved here with the triumph of Hitler in the 1930s. Few of us asked questions about their past or present convictions because we took for granted that they had left either in fear of persecution or to make a brave protest. They were our kind of folks. It took me a long time to find out that many of them had strange histories and that their hosts, or the people who vouched for them, knew all about their past. Two of the perhaps eight or nine that I met turned out to have unexpected reasons for emigration: both had been Nazi sympathizers.... [B]y 1938 I had been through the life and death of my friend Julia, and had been to Spain during the Civil War, and had been moved by men willing to die for what they believed in. (*Pentimento,* 487–88)

In *Watch on the Rhine,* Hellman once again restricts her exploration to a single set, a *lieu de mémoire* whose geographical location just outside Washington, D.C. indicates Hellman's concern with "the process of cultural recovery," a notion advocated by Melvin Dixon in "The Black Writer's Use of Memory."[28] Dixon's essay focuses on "the way geographic locations such

---

26 Falk, 68.
27 *Ibid.,* 69. Notes on European events can be found in the University of Texas collection for *Watch on the Rhine.*
28 *History and Memory in African-American Culture,* ed. Genevieve Fabre and Robert O'Meally (New York & Oxford: Oxford UP, 1994), 19.

as the American South and Africa have become important sites of memory in the construction of a viable African American culture," which is an extrapolation of Nora's notion that memory becomes a tool to regain and reconstruct not just the past but history itself. Hellman utilizes the same technique in choosing the farm country near the nation's capital of Washington, D.C. The invasion of Europeans into an American living room serves to juxtapose American and European values as Hellman examines the present state of America's proclaimed egalitarian belief in justice.

> I wanted to write a play about nice, liberal Americans whose lives would be shaken up by Europeans, by a world the new Fascists had won because the old values had long been dead. I put the play in a small Ohio town. That didn't work at all.... [T]hen I moved the play to Washington, placed it in the house of a rich, liberal family who were about to meet their anti-fascist son-in-law, a German, who had fought in Spain. (*Pentimento*, 487–89)

Hence, the mansion itself is a site wrapped up with "a heap of signifying" regarding the vitality of past values and need for American cultural recovery.

The "living room of the Farrelly house, about twenty miles from Washington, D.C." presents itself on a warm spring morning, an auspicious time for rebirth and growth.[29] Built in the early nineteenth century, inhabited by four or five generations of people of taste who've furnished the room in no particular style or period, but with objects of many times and places whose only common denominator is that they were liked by the careless aristocrats who possessed them, the Farrelly country house becomes a metaphor for America's relatively short history compared to Europe and the American elite's current neglect of traditional values. The Farrellys are aristocrats in the American sense. Well-educated and cultured, socially prominent, they are an "old" family of five generations containing judges, lawyers, and diplomats who could trace their roots to the American Revolution. Hence, theirs is a well-established connection to the seat of government as well as to the heart of America in their love for the country, the land and garden belonging to the farm. In contrast to *The Little Foxes*, we are in a world of old money and influence and love for the land itself.

In a deft touch reminiscent of Ibsen's portrait of the general in *Hedda Gabler*, Hellman hangs the painting of "kind-faced" Joshua Farrelly, famous American judge, on the living room wall. Ibsen concerns himself with the dying Norwegian aristocracy and the termination of its line in the suicide of Hedda Gabler; Hellman's focus is the power of comfortable self-interest to

---

[29] Lillian Hellman, *Watch on the Rhine*, 205.

blind its possessors, however well-meaning, to the existence of tyrannical oppression. Hellman, like Joshua Farrelly, is concerned that

> the complete American is dying.... A complete man... is a man who wants to know. He wants to know how fast a bird can fly, how thick is the crust of the earth, what made Iago evil, how to plow a field. He knows there is no dignity to a mountain if there is no dignity to man. You can't put that in a man, but when it's there put your trust in him. (261)

She identifies Kurt, the German anti-fascist, with Joshua when he quotes from his father-in law's letter:

> "I am getting older now and Europe seems far away. Fanny and I will have an early breakfast on the porch and then I shall drive the boys into Washington." And then he goes on: "Henry Adams tells me he has been reading Karl Marx. I shall have to tell him my father made me read Marx many years ago and that, since he proposes to impress me, will spoil Henry's Sunday." (225–26)

Joshua's interest in Marx parallels Kurt's socialist, as opposed to fascist, value system and provides an answer to Bodo's inquiry about the unequal distribution of worldly goods among the populace.

Hellman's characteristic technique of invading the stage space occurs once again in *Watch on the Rhine*. She brings Hitler's invasion home—even the house bells sound like air raid alarms. The Balkan nobility are the first invaders: Teck and Marthe de Brancovis have already moved in. Kurt's American wife Sara recognizes Teck as the fascist he is:

> We know how many there are of you. They don't, yet. My mother and brother feel shocked that you are in their house. For us—we have seen you in so many houses. (257)

At the play's opening, the hilariously funny matriarch concerns herself with the gossip of diplomatic circles. She bosses around her French and African American servants and her 39-year-old bachelor lawyer son David, who flirts with the married Countess. The comedy of manners throws the significance of the *lieu de mémoire* into relief. Fanny Farrelly's great excitement over the imminent arrival of the Mueller family—her daughter Sara, German son-in-law Kurt, and three grandchildren she has never met—overwhelms the dangerous presence of the Brancovises under her own roof and emphasizes a sense of being on the cusp of change. When the Muellers arrive, we are aware of both their financial and physical difficulties—evident in Sara's dowdy old clothes, the children's delight in a real breakfast, and Kurt's bodily weakness from injuries inflicted by the Nazis to his face and hands. We discover that Kurt uses the excuse of seeking a vacation with his wife's fam-

ily to cover his real mission of carrying funds to support the resistance
movement in Germany. Kurt is a man of action, much stronger than Horace
who, weak from heart disease, wishes to retreat from the voracious Hubbards. Hellman reinforces Kurt's dedication to the ideal of freedom with his
past participation in the Spanish Civil War. Serving on the anti-fascist side in
the German Brigade defending the bridge over the Manzanares River in
1936, Kurt transforms the old World War One German song into a defiant
declaration against "the bastards who sell the blood of other men." Sara and
Fanny link Kurt's defense of democratic principles with those of Joshua Farrelly, the man in the portrait as well as the man of the house (238–39).

> KURT: We did fight but we did not win. It would have been a different world
> if we had.
>   SARA: Papa said so years ago. Do you remember, Mama? "For every man who
> lives without freedom, the rest of us must face the guilt."
>   FANNY: Yes. "We are liable in the conscience-balance for the tailor in Lodz,
> the black man in our South, the peasant in— " *(Turns to Teck. Unpleasantly.)* Your
> country, perhaps. (238–39)

Teck de Brancovis, however, does not support the Farrelly/Mueller point of
view. Once the symbol of culture and class, this former Romanian diplomat
is a down-at-heels refugee, gambler, and Nazi sympathizer who is "a man
selling the lives of other men" (255). He has no intention of remaining in
America to build a better, free life as previous refugees did, but blackmails
Kurt to garner a return visa to Nazi Germany.

The clash between Kurt and Teck is the play's climax, the explosive
moment of danger in which the hero takes action. The fictional dramatic conflict suggests opposition and resistance to the current historical event of fascist invasion. Once again, Hellman brings violence into the living room as
she did in *Days to Come* and *The Little Foxes*. Kurt attacks Teck and drags
his body out to the terrace to kill him. With the murder, Kurt de-rails the Farrelly attempt to buy Teck off and consequently they must decide whether to
be accomplices to Kurt's deed. Significantly, Hellman does not let things
stand with Fanny's offer to give Kurt the money she planned to give Teck,
but demands that all the Farrellys—representative of the American judicial
system—support his escape and return to continue the anti-fascist movement
in Germany. She, however, does not condone the notion of killing unless essential human dignity is denied, as it was in the Nazi murder of 27 men in the
Kirchweih festival of August 1931. A brutal event like this one—attacking
poor survivors of World War I—creates "a man who might fight to make a
good world" (263). Like Kurt, Americans cannot afford to be passive any
longer. The Farrellys may have had an old friendship with Alfonso of Spain,

whose autographed photo sits in the living room (215), but myopic negligence allows violent oppression to expand (World War I to the Spanish Civil War to World War II). Kurt finally answers Bodo's question to Teck—"comfort and plenty exist. Yet all cannot have them. Why?" (229)—with action against fascism's creation of overweening self-interest in an elitist Aryan society.

The play contains yet another form of invasion and revolution. The subplot utilizing the Teck/Marthe/David triangle lends itself to an examination of the institution of marriage, itself a paradigm for the mores of society at large. Kurt and Sara's is a love match, not a social arrangement. Initially opposed but later endorsed by Fanny, their mutual affection reflects that of the senior Farrellys and contrasts with the bitter relationship of the Count and Countess de Brancovis. Hellman gives us a Sara whose anti-fascist political stance finds its expression in her loving support of Kurt's need to return to Germany to rescue Max Freidank, an actual historical person in the anti-fascist movement!

Teck de Brancovis manipulated his social status to invade the top stratum of American society in marrying Marthe Randolph. Her mother, a member of Washington's elite and a friend of Fanny, forced her daughter into the type of society marriage with a dashing European aristocrat so scrutinized in the novels of Henry James (242). Marthe's loveless arrangement is further testimony to the destructive results of marriage for wealth and status and to a fear of resistance against the *status quo*. At the opening of the play, the Balkan nobility have been sponging off the Farrellys for weeks. Penalized for taking the anti-fascist side in a Budapest oil deal (257), Teck gambles with Nazi sympathizer and aristocrat Phili von Seitz at the German embassy to curry favor. Marthe has recognized his opportunism for some time, but when he uses the Farrellys' home and Kurt to further his own interests, she breaks off their marriage and aligns herself with the man she loves, David Farrelly. Significantly, the Marthe/Teck split occurs in the living room in front of Sara, David, and Fanny. Marthe's decision is another kind of American Revolution, a choice Regina Giddens was unable to make. For Hellman, convictions inspire action, not just talk.

> SARA: I just don't like polite political conversations.
> TECK: All of us, in Europe had too many of them.
> SARA: Yes. Too much talk. By this time all of us know where we are and what we have to do. It's an indulgence to sit in a room and discuss your beliefs as if they were the afternoon's golf game—
> FANNY: You know, Sara, I find it very pleasant that Kurt, considering his history doesn't make platform speeches. He hasn't tried to convince anybody of anything.

> SARA: Why should he, Mama? You are quite old enough to have your own convictions—or Papa's.
> FANNY: *(turns to look at her.)* I am proud to have Papa's convictions.
> SARA: Of course. But it might be well to have a few new ones, now and then. (230–31)

Now that the magnolias have been shaken, Fanny and David help Kurt to leave the country to continue "the fight to make a good world" in Germany (263). Fanny finally admits Marthe Armstrong into her own home after recognizing Marthe's honest love for David as well as her need to rid herself of the parasitic fascist Teck.

The Searching Wind

In *The Searching Wind* (1944), Hellman pushes beyond the story of a heroic anti-fascist resisting National Socialism in Germany and the involvement of an upper-class American family in his direct assistance. She moves to an outright condemnation of America's pursuit of an appeasement policy towards the Fascists during World War II. Hellman's utilization of specific European historical events throughout the play enables the presentation of contrasting points of view as heard from those who were soldiers at the front, those in the diplomatic corps working on international treaties, or journalists trying to inform Americans at home.

The play's title comes from an expression used by Helen, Hellman's African American housekeeper: "It takes a searching wind to find the tree you sit in."[30] The idiom means "Who can tell what side you are on if you don't know your own mind?" and refers to the "confused, unformulated upperclass liberal attitude toward racism."[31] Hellman extends its usage in the play to comment on the weakness, however well-meaning, of America's approach towards the rise of Fascism in Italy, Germany, and France. Not content with the exposure of Fascist sympathizers on American soil, she focuses on an American diplomatic family and its failure to act when confronted by actual historical events. Her condemnation of the policy of appeasement is reinforced by illustrating its failure at key moments of danger housed in a new European setting. Despite his refusal to accept villainy in a manner not unlike Andrew Rodman, diplomat Alex Hazen's *modus operandi* of playing the dangerous game of "working with what there is to work with" is put to the test.[32] Allowing the Fascists to put down the Communist revolutionaries in

---

[30] Lillian Hellman, *An Unfinished Woman*, 252.
[31] Falk, 70.
[32] Lillian Hellman, *The Searching Wind*, 279.

Italy and Germany has its parallels in Rodman's acceptance of Ellicott's thug-like strikebreakers in *Days to Come*. However, when it comes to the ambitious thrust towards control of Europe by Hitler and Mussolini, the policy of appeasement fails to stop the fascist advance every time. In the play a major explosive historical event occurs immediately after an appeasing action onstage. *The Searching Wind*, while formally innovative, is one of Hellman's weakest dramas because of the essential difficulty in wrapping a play's story around passive characters in an overwhelmingly active situation. Well-meaning individuals who fail to take decisive action also fail to capture the interest of an audience.

When considering *The Searching Wind* as a *lieu de mémoire*, we must look at Hellman's use of settings once again. Unlike her other plays, *The Searching Wind* employs a combination of multiple settings and multiple time periods: scenes in the present (1944) and flashbacks (1922, 1923, and 1938). Using a "You are there!" approach (later adapted by television news), Hellman takes the audience to earlier scenes of conflict—Mussolini's 1922 invasion of Rome, the Freikorps attack on Jews during inflationary 1923, and Berlin and the signing of the 1938 Munich Pact, which Alex Hazen recognizes as "a complete capitulation to Hitler and "the beginning of a world war" (318). Alex, however, vacillates between protesting "further German aggressions" and protecting his son Sam under the cover of the possibility of "a generation kept from war and the sparing of our sons" (318). Moses Taney, Alex's father-in-law and an armchair liberal, sees the truth, but doesn't report the actual facts to his own newspaper.

> All we can do is compromise. Compromise and compromise. There's nothing like a good compromise to cost a few million men their lives. Well, I'm glad I retired. I don't like having anything to do with the death of other people. Sad world, eh, Alex? *(The door slams. Moses smiles.)* (319)

More than in any other play, the cinematic treatment allows Hellman to intensify the dangerous nature of current American isolationist self-interest to long-held American democratic ideals, particularly those of free speech and equal justice. Hellman anchors the play in the drawing room of the Hazen house located in the nation's capital, Washington, D.C. and home to a family of longterm professional career diplomats. Instead of the Farrelly portrait on the wall, Hellman frames two living people in a "room of fine proportions with good furniture, good pictures and good ornament" (271). The surroundings indicate excellent quality, wealth, and a general neutrality. The living room/terrace combination reminds us of the usual Hellman set. However when Hellman presents 70-year-old Moses Taney, retired liberal newspaper publisher, and his grandson 20-year-old Corporal Samuel Hazen, a

disabled vet home from the Italian Front, she brings to life the ongoing debate about the value of American participation in the war within the luxurious, insulated surroundings of the Hazen household where people still dress
for dinner. Both are reading newspapers containing Alex Hazen's impressions of Africa and Southern Italy, yet Sam has difficulty relating the article
to his own experience at the Italian front (in the same way that Alex couldn't
describe his fighting experience in France to his own father). Moses hates the
"diplomatic double-talk" that comes

> from a long line of men who've meddled in the affairs of this country. ...and believe
> that,... sometimes democracies have to deal with people they don't approve and
> sometimes in order to save something or other, you have to do something else or
> other. (276; 272)

We learn quickly that newspapers, *lieux de mémoire* themselves, often do not
report the truth, but serve those in power. Taney's cynical world-weariness is
not easily understood by the young, wounded soldier whose multilingual
background and Harvard education haven't served to protect him from the
realities of war—the death of his friend Leck the baker and his own leg in-
jury. While Sam believes that "children of famous fathers and famous grand-
fathers" may "learn to walk late," he reminds Moses about Leck's death and
brings forth a key apology from Moses:

> Sorry, sorry Sam. At my age you forget what's important and... and remember what
> isn't. *(Points to the newspaper.)* I can almost remember the words in which your
> father and I talked about this same Victor Emmanuel gentleman twenty-two years
> ago, the day Mussolini marched into Rome. (279)

Before segueing to this very time and place in the next scene, Hellman
exposes the hypocrisy found in the liberal establishment. Mussolini's invasion of Rome occurs on the very day Moses Taney retired from the newspaper and relinquished his responsibility to report the real story behind the
news. Sam questions Moses about the paper's poor reporting and asks Moses
how he could not care about delivering the news. In 1944, Moses, whose
name refers to the Biblical leader of the chosen people, cynically views
newspapers as the vehicle through which dilettantes continue "acting important and misinforming folks." Moses deems the newspaper unsuitable employment for Sam, who, as in the Bible, becomes the play's judge and
thereby a successor to Zan. Ironically, Moses, the guardian of free speech,
refuses to speak out *in print*.

As in *Watch on the Rhine*, Hellman also allows the conservative European perspective sympathetic to the Nazis to invade the living room. Ponette,
a recent French émigré and former store owner in Toulouse, resents being

reduced in status to Hazen's butler and his wife to their cook. He blames the French premier Léon Blum whose Socialist Party (and Jewish religion) and his strike-supporting relatives for the German invasion that requires his flight to America. The Hazens' black housekeeper Sophronia compares Ponette, whose wife had a servant of her own, with every Southerner's claim that he came from a family ruined by the Civil War. She observes that "Now there's never a refugee who wasn't rich." When Emily declares that Sophronia doesn't like their refugees, Moses agrees with her, remarking that "No old American stock likes foreigners. Narrow of us" (274–75).

Before taking us to a new location, Hellman introduces the Hazens. Alex the diplomat works with the old men who represent the governments-in-exile even if you don't "always like them or trust them," the same argument used in 1922 by President Wilson (League of Nations) and France's Clemenceau, as Mussolini took over Rome (279–80). Emily, Moses' daughter and wife of Alex, is part of the "ambassadoring" couple. Despite her liberal background, she hobnobs with European high society sympathetic to Mussolini at the Hayworths. Both are compromisers in that Alex will do anything to prevent war and Emily will run with a similar, "cultured" social set regardless of their political affiliations.

Emily also introduces the subplot. Although she had stolen Alex from her former schoolfriend Cassie, Emily invites the "other woman" Cassie Bowman to dinner after a twenty-year hiatus. Moses jokingly compares their meeting to the reconciliation of General Grant and General Lee, an event which never occurred in the Civil War. Nor does appeasement work here. Alex Hazen may want both women in his life, but Emily won't continue this way. Unfortunately, the play never pits the two women against each other or shoves Alex into the fray. The lack of onstage confrontation in personal relationships simply echoes the lack of confrontation between America and the Fascists on the international level.

Scene 2 is *The Searching Wind*'s first European *lieu de mémoire*. The setting is the living room of a suite in the Grand Hotel, Rome. Again we have the anonymity of a hotel room which could be inhabited by anyone who has the money to rent it. Packing trunks in the middle of the room notify the audience of impending evacuation and the opening phone call from Alex suggests escape first to the embassy and then to the boat. Meanwhile there is gunfire in the background. Moses insists the family stay at the hotel despite the ambassador's offer of refuge at the embassy. The atmosphere of imminent danger is set.

Two Italian waiters come in with elaborate room service. The older one relays the manager's message that no guests have anything to worry about in

Rome; the younger one coughs from war injuries. Sophronia perceives the underlying fear of invasion. Moses, newspaperman at the time, reads from the ticker tape: "The government is in control. King Victor Emmanuel returned this morning from bathing in the sea. The stories of Mussolini's armies are lies. He is not marching on the city. But everybody is to stay off the streets in case he is—" (284). Moses recognizes that the gunfire is a fake show put on by government guns shooting in the air and predicts Mussolini's advance into the city in a few hours. The young Italian waiter reveals that the King and the Government side with the Fascisti, who are also supported by many foreigners and the hotel residents. When Taney confesses that he knew this about a year ago, but asks himself why he didn't see it coming sooner, the young waiter says that many Italians saw it coming when President Wilson came to speak to the Italian people three years earlier. Wilson never did, but spent his time with the "great names" within the palace while masses of ordinary people waited outside. Moses condemns Wilson as a "man who likes fancy words and fancy names," but does nothing. Meanwhile Emily has been hobnobbing with a set of socialites (Hayworths, Perrone, etc.) who say the Fascisti will mean "a recovery for Italy." Cassie ironically suggests that they believe they would return to Rome the "glory of Caesar," that is, return Italy to its Imperial Age and keep the wealthy in positions of power (286). A far cry from the poverty-stricken, strike-riven land they now inhabit. What Cassie does not realize is that Emily will remain in Rome, playing the piano just as Nero played the violin, to capture Alex for herself.

The manager arrives to insure their protection. When Cassie confronts Alex about American involvement, he lets Cassie know that the Ambassador is "here to represent the United States and not to fight in civil wars." Cassie does not understand the lack of involvement and says "We're an ignorant generation. We see so much and know so little. Maybe because we think about ourselves so much" (289). Despite their declared love for each other, Cassie rejects Alex's "embassy" perspective and decides to go home to think everything through. Just as Alex is about to kiss her, Moses interrupts, joking that even though people may have kissed during the French Revolution, they can take their personal business to the lobby. By identifying the turmoil in Italy with the French revolution, Taney sees evidence of a class struggle.

Suddenly the war outside enters the room, as two fascist soldiers propelling the manager before them burst in just as the ticker tape announces King Victor Emmanuel's request to Mussolini to form a government. The union of aristocracy and Fascisti has occurred. Calling them swine, Taney turns on the soldiers. Alex steps in and defends him using the American Embassy as a shield. Alex, though, has returned to the hotel room for a purpose—to talk

Taney out of making a strong newspaper statement against the Fascists. He says: "Any statement you give will be dangerous to the relations between our country and Italy. The Ambassador feels that we cannot take sides in an internal uprising—" (291–92). When Taney rejects Alex's plea, Alex explains where he stands:

> I can only speak for myself. I don't like this, and I don't like your thinking I do. But another few months of the kind of misery and starvation they've had, and there would have been a revolution. If Mussolini can put it down that doesn't make me like him, or the money behind him, or the people. But somebody had to do it, and you don't pick gentlemen to do the job. You were at the Peace Conference and you know that wasn't wild talk about Communism in Italy.... And now I am going to tell you, Mr. Taney, that with all your liberal beliefs, I do not believe that you want that. (292)

Moses replies: "That's well said, and mostly true. But I didn't want this and I have fought hard, in my way, to stop it. I don't like to see people put down by gangsters who make a job of doing it for those who want it done..." (292). Choosing the lesser of two evils, Taney promises not to write anything for the paper and in fact to quit journalism. He subscribes to the notion that Fascism, supported by the power elite, eliminates the spectre of a successful communist revolution. "Politics makes strange bedfellows." The play continues to explore the consequences of America's willingness to compromise.

Scene 3 takes us back to 1944 in the Hazen drawing room a few hours later than Scene 1. After dinner with his parents, Sam continues his education.

> SAM: I was thinking that you often know more about people in books than—than I've known about any of you, I guess. *(To Alex.)* I didn't know you had been in Italy when Fascism first started. There you were on such a big day and it was so important how you figured out that day. Or maybe I think so because I was there and saw what it did—*(Lamely.)* I can't seem to say what I mean.
>
> ALEX: You mean that if people like me had seen it straight, maybe you wouldn't have had to be there twenty-two years later. (296)

Emily and Moses hedge by talking about the difficulty of seeing their own time clearly, but Sam is determined to "learn how to put things together." The scene drifts to Alex questioning Cassie about why she came to dinner and Emily insisting Cassie stay to discuss what happened since 1922. Since Alex admits that it is a rare man who sees his own time as "clearly as if it were history," Hellman, with the added benefit of hindsight, will enable Sam to do just that by the end of the play.

Act Two, Scene 1, takes us to the corner of a restaurant in 1923 Berlin. A discussion between Hazen and the owner Eppler reflects the raging inflation in Germany where a loaf of bread now costs 140 billion marks. Hazen and

tourists can use foreign currency to buy food, but the Germans, struggling
from reparations ordered by the Versailles Treaty, resent foreigners. The
sudden eruption of a riot outside disrupts the conversation and establishes the
volatility of desperate poverty. Led by the Freikorps—the demobilized right-
wing, volunteer troops who banded together to smash riots, retain order in
the streets, and prevent Germany from becoming a Bolshevik regime—the
mob attacks a group of elderly Jews. Hazen attempts to calm down other
people in the restaurant:

> I am Hazen of the American Embassy. Herr Eppler wishes me to tell you that there
> has been a disgraceful riot of hoodlums against the Jewish section. The police tell
> him that it is under control. In any case, it is not near here, but the doors must be
> kept closed until he is allowed to open them. Mr. Eppler asks you to go on with your
> lunch. There is nothing to be done now except by the police. (300)

Hazen does not immediately recognize the collusion of police and Freikorps. Cassie surprises him with her accurate description of the event as a
"pogrom" (301). Then his new wife Emily appears and describes driving
across the Judenstrasse and witnessing both attacks on Jews and Americans
who were told to "mind [their] own business" (302). The young American
Halsey puts it all in perspective:

> The Freikorps people are in on it. I think its real leaders came from the Young Peo-
> ple's League, just as they did last week. There's no question now it's tied up with
> the Bavarian trouble. The story around is that somebody from Thyssen put up the
> money for Ludendorff and for those clowns outside. (302)

The Young People's League is of course the Nazi Youth organization.
Thyssen is the big German steel manufacturer. Ludendorff was Hindenburg's
Chief of Staff in the battles against the Russians in the Great War. The Ba-
varian trouble, Hitler's National Socialism, ties it all together. Yet Alex can't
accept the facts. He says: "That's hard to believe. He's a bad guy, but nobody's bad enough to put up the money for this." Cassie tells him the truth:
"Dear Alex. You haven't changed. Nobody's that bad, even when the proof
is outside the door" (302). The strongest action Alex suggests is to go to the
police and make a strong official protest on the grounds that many Americans are in Berlin (303). After Alex leaves with Halsey, the two women are
left to discuss the situation of one stealing the other's beau and end up part-
ing with no solution to the antagonism in sight. Unfortunately, the most exciting action in the scene occurs offstage.

Scene 2 takes us to the Hotel Meurice suite in 1938 just as Paris is being
evacuated before a possible German invasion. Alex, now the American ambassador, still "can't believe in villainy" (307). Count von Stammer, an en-

voy from Von Ribbentrop, the German foreign minister of the Nazi regime, attempts to influence Alex to oppose any French declaration of war or any resistance to Hitler's wish to take the Sudetenland. He suggests a deal in which the British and French will give it to Hitler to turn Hitler's attention away from Europe towards an attack on Russia. The evacuation of Paris and mobilization are simply ploys by the governments to "frighten the people out of a war" (310). Revolted by the duplicity and "deals of war," Alex can't believe "any other democracy" would consider bartering away another country's rights, whether it be the Sudetenland or Czechoslovakia. His ambivalent actions betray him, however. Alex arranges a rendezvous with his old lover Cassie, and voices his rage about Emily's financial dealings with people and banks affiliated with the Nazis and Japanese. Emily, however, plays her winning card when she pleads for Sam's life. A radio announcement from London says that Prime Minister Chamberlain and Premier Daladier will fly to Munich, and Alex knows the ceding of the Sudetenland to Hitler is a foregone conclusion. Debating his report, he asks the question foremost in Hellman's mind:

> What the hell has one man got to do with history? There's something crazy about sitting here and thinking that what I say makes any difference. What do I know? What does anybody know? What the hell could they do at home, anyway? (317)

Finally he sits down to write:

> It is my belief—earnest belief that we should protest against any further German aggressions or against any further concessions to them. But I am convinced that Mr. Chamberlain is working in the interests of peace and his actions must not be judged too sharply. If he can save his sons and our sons from war.... (317)

While Alex sees the Munich Pact as a complete capitulation and as the beginning of a world war, he still proposes no action and thereby becomes Count von Stammer's accomplice. Ultimately, this immediate compromise will bring about the deaths of millions and a reprimand from the very son whose life he was trying to save.

Scene 3 takes us back to the Hazen house about an hour after Scene 3 of Act One. Cassie admits to taking revenge on Emily for marrying Alex and recognizes the "frivolous nature of all three of them, a generation of people who didn't know what they were doing or why they did it " (320). On the heels of Cassie's departure, Sam confronts his father with his recommendation of appeasement the day before Munich (321) and his grandfather with his belief that history is only made by the masses of people as an excuse "to just sit back and watch" (322). Sam goes on to read the newspaper clipping describing his mother at a fancy dinner party with Nazi sympathizers, a betrayal of American values. Sam reveals what his friend Leck said to him at the front:

> Sam, that banker the piece talked about, he used to deal with the Germans before it got too hot. He's a no good guy. And the rest of those people, they're all old tripe who just live in our country now and pretend they are on the right side. When the trouble came in their countries they sold out their people and beat it quick, and now they make believe they're all for everything good. My God, Sam... if you come from that you better get away from it fast, because they made the shit we're sitting in. (324)

Sam, however, does not sit back and watch. He willingly fought to free Italy from Fascism at Bloody Basin and reveals the coming amputation of his leg as a result. He—like Kurt, Zan, and Dashiell Hammett—believes in standing up for his ideals.

> How do you say you like your country? I like this place. *(With great passion.)* And I don't want any more fancy fooling around with it. I don't want any more of Father's mistakes, for any reason, good or bad, or yours, Mother, because I think they do it harm. I was ashamed of that clipping. But I didn't really know why. I found out tonight. I am ashamed of both of you, and that's the truth. I don't want to be ashamed that way again. I don't like losing my leg, I don't like losing it at all. I'm scared—but everybody's welcome to it as long as it means a little something and helps to bring us out someplace. All right. I've said enough. Let's have a drink. (324)

Hellman rewrites history in *The Searching Wind* by using actual explosive events leading up to and during World War II. She plunges her characters and her audience into the midst of the European war zone. However, instead of thrusting her characters directly into the conflict, she reveals their naïveté, self-interest, and unwillingness to take action when faced with the oppressive force of fascism. Historical events surround neutral, luxurious living spaces and throw into relief the failure of all-too-comfortable Americans to live up to the Founding Fathers' belief in equal justice and opportunity for all.

CHAPTER FOUR

August Wilson: Talking History

Wilson retains his hometown neighborhood as the location of all of his plays except *Ma Rainey's Black Bottom*, set in Chicago. His Hill District community becomes a kind of extended family whose experiences and narratives define the evolution of the new black man with roots in Africa and dreams in America and simultaneously expand the face of American history itself. Wilson spins this urban cocoon to allow his black folk to freely express themselves to an audience both black and white and to protect against an ever-threatening white economic and judicial system with its attendant violence. Only twice in his plays to date does killing actually occur—once in the neighborhood (*Seven Guitars*) and once in the white man's recording studio (*Ma Rainey's Black Bottom*). Interestingly enough, where money and cultural commodification come into play, black man attacks black man regardless of setting in a misplaced attack on his own, instead of on those responsible for his sense of worthlessness and powerlessness.

> ...in 1982, when I began to write plays in earnest, I would become involved in the idea of history by proposing to write a play that dealt with black life and manners for each decade of the 20th century.
>
> ....
>
> I soon discovered, however, that I was as interested in the culture as in the history. I found what to me was the culture's greatest expression in the blues, and began my historical explorations by uncovering the ideas and attitudes so important to my characters. Since I was not a historian but a writer of fiction, I saw as my task the invention of characters. These personal histories would not only represent the culture but illuminate the historical context both of the period in which the play is set and the continuum of black life in American (sic) that stretches back to the early 17th century.
>
> I was encouraged by the fact that in all my reading of history, seldom, if ever, was the black experience and presence in America given any historical weight, seldom were they admitted to the larger playing field of cause and effect. I sought then to simply restore that experience to a primary role, thereby giving the facts of history a different perspective, and creating, in essence, a world in which the black American was the spiritual center.[1]

---

[1] *New York Times* 4/12/92, p. 5—Section 2; Column 3; Arts & Leisure.

August Wilson brings the past into the present of his plays to give voice to those previously considered historyless and simultaneously combines his literary construction of history with a journey of self-discovery:[2]

> It's my story. I claim it—all four hundred years of it. I claim the right to tell it in any way I choose because it's, in essence, my autobiography; only it's my autobiography of myself and my ancestors.

In this context, Wilson's memory becomes "the poet's chief means of writing the self into the larger history of the race"[3] and the community becomes a site "on which the drama of self-acquisition is played."[4] In his dramas, Wilson establishes a community cocoon which provides a secure, safe environment for the free expression of African American culture through anecdotal history, "the trope of the talking book" as described by Henry Louis Gates, Jr., in *The Signifying Monkey* (127–69), and an insider's view of appropriate character behavior. These seemingly spontaneous tales of "the distinct rupture in black family genealogy" from the Middle Passage to the play's period combined with contemporary dramatic action are meant to be heard ("loud talking") and seen by both the black and white audience. As Wilson says: "If you go into the black community, you have the culture of black America still very much alive. They still practice the values that their grandparents had, with some exceptions, of course...."[5] Wilson practices a "strategy of recollection" for reconstructing not only the past but history itself.

Wilson places this odyssey of cultural recovery and the affirmation of self within specific stage settings which operate like Nora's *lieux de mémoire*. Wilson shares Melvin Dixon's notion of geographic locations, such as the northern urban community of Harlem or the American South or Africa, as important sites of memory in the construction of a viable African American culture. Dixon writes:

> These sites have been used by many African American writers not only to evoke a sense of place, but, more importantly, to enlarge the frame of cultural reference for the depiction of black experiences by anchoring that experience in memory—a memory that ultimately rewrites history. (20)

---

2   Sandra D. Shannon, *The Dramatic Vision of August Wilson* (Washington, DC: Howard UP, 1995), 203.

3   Melvin Dixon, "The Black Writer's Use of Memory," in Genevieve Fabre and Robert O'Meally, eds., *History and Memory in African-American Culture* (New York: Oxford UP, 1994), 26.

4   Dixon, 21.

5   *New York Times* 4/12/92, p. 5—Section 2; Column 3; Arts & Leisure.

Wilson's stage settings, all but one located in the Hill District of his hometown of Pittsburgh, are "jealously protected enclaves"[6] privileging and protecting African American memory and thereby act as a material trace of
black history in America. The specific theatrical environments, in their historical detail and metaphorical significance, become part of Wilson's "strategy of recollection" for reconstructing not only the past but history itself. In
all but one of his plays, *Ma Rainey's Black Bottom*, Wilson takes us inside
his own community, reveals its hopes, virtues and problems, and simultaneously interrogates the African American role within a larger white-dominated
society.

Ma Rainey's Black Bottom

August Wilson layers *lieux de mémoire* in *Ma Rainey's Black Bottom* in
the greater locale of 1927 Chicago, in the blues, in the actual historical figure
Ma Rainey, and in the stage setting of a period recording studio where white
men both exploit and attempt to alter black music to make a profit. Significantly, Wilson moves to Chicago in the Twenties, the destination city of
many blacks leaving the poverty-ridden South for factory jobs in the North
and the pulsating magnet for blues singers to its clubs and recording studios.
Ma Rainey's Chicago of 1927 is a rough city embracing

> millionaires and derelicts, gangsters and roughhouse dandies, whores and Irish
> grandmothers...secretaries, priest and altarboys from St. Anthony's church, stock-
> yards and busboys in Mac's Place cleaning away the last of the corned beef and
> cabbage.[7]

In the midst of the hubbub Wilson foregrounds his specific subject matter,
his black characters:

> on the city's South Side, sleepy-eyed negroes move lazily toward their small cold-
> water flats and rented rooms to await the onslaught of night, which will find them
> crowded in the bars and jukejoints both dazed and dazzling in their rapport with life.
> It is with these negroes that our concern lies most heavily: their values, their atti-
> tudes, and particularly their music. (xv)

In this play, Wilson first voices his "blues ideology" that presents the
music as both a connector and a way of life, a *lieu de mémoire* containing the
roots, conscience, and means of expression and reassembly for the black
man. He writes:

---

6   Nora, 289.
7   August Wilson, *Ma Rainey's Black Bottom,* xv.

I think that the music has a cultural response of black Americans to the world they find themselves in. Blues is the best literature we have. If you look at the singers, they actually follow a long line all the way back to Africa and various other parts of the world. They are people who are carriers of the culture, carriers of the ideas—the troubadours in Europe, etc. Except in black America—in this society—they were not valued except among the black folks who understood. I've always thought of them as sacred because of the sacred tasks they had taken upon themselves to disseminate this information and carry these cultural values of the people. And I found that white America would very often abuse them. I don't think that it was without purpose in the sense that the blues and music have always been at the forefront in the development of the character and consciousness of black America, and people have senselessly destroyed that or stopped that. Then you're taking away from the people their self-definition—in essence, their self-determination. These guys were arrested as vagrants and drunkards and whatever. They were never seen as valuable members of a society by whites.[8]

Wilson's heroine Ma Rainey voices the importance of the blues to black culture:

> MA RAINEY: It keeps things balanced…. White folks don't understand about the blues. They hear it come out, but they don't know how it got there. They don't understand that's life's way of talking. You don't sing to feel better. You sing cause that's a way of understanding life.
> CUTLER: that's right. You get that understanding and you done got a grip on life to where you can hold your head up and go on to see what else life got to offer. (82–83)

To blacks torn apart from their families during the Middle Passage, slavery, Reconstruction, and northward emigration, the blues become the artery of connection and expression.

> MA RAINEY: The blues help you get out of bed in the morning. You get up knowing you ain't alone. There's something else in the world. Something's been added by that song. This be an empty world without the blues. I take that emptiness and try to fill it up with something.
> TOLEDO: You fill it up with something the people can't be without, Ma. That's why they call you the Mother of the Blues. (83)

In 1927 Blues music is itself changing from country "jug band music" to urban dance music. This development is both a response to the new African American urban life style, but also to the music's popularity with the white man, the traditional source of money. Wilson sees African American culture under attack from the white man who wants to exploit it to his own financial

---

8   Shannon, 204–205.

advantage and from blacks themselves who do not recognize its unique value.

Wilson deliberately chooses an environment in which the white man is in control. In *Ma Rainey*, the larger social context finds its metaphorical expression in the one setting which, out of all of his dramas, is *not* located within Wilson's Pittsburgh Hill District. Power rests primarily with him and secondarily with Ma Rainey who, while refusing to accommodate the white man's demand to revamp her music, still sells him "property rights" to it and, by extension, to African American culture.

The play's triple-layered building is a vertical structure that metaphorically represents the hierarchical organization of American society. The top stratum is the control booth inhabited and operated by the white producer Sturdyvant, whose Dutch name reflects his European ancestry and links him to early American settlement. He is "preoccupied with money and insensitive to black performers" (17) whom he deals with at a distance, i.e. from the control booth. The mid-level recording studio is the designated place for black/white interaction. Here Ma Rainey, Dussie, Sylvester and the band members meet up with Ma's white manager Irvin, "who prides himself on his knowledge of blacks and his ability to deal with them" (17), though he never invites them to his house. His job is to record black music for mass consumption to earn lots of money for himself and Sturdyvant. However, the recording studio is not a calm interface between black and white, but the allowable corridor for blacks to produce a commodity for whites to buy and for whites to produce inexpensively a profitable product. This second stratum is also subject to invasion by the police, whose harassment keeps blacks in line in the larger society. The basement level is the band room where the "leftovers of history" (57)—the black musicians now freed from slavery—practice in the midst of miscellaneous furniture, piano, lockers, mirror, posters, and other forgotten paraphernalia just like them.

Unlike the settings of Wilson's other plays, this building belongs to the white hegemony. Consequently, when a white man sets foot in the middle zone of the studio, issues of control arise; after he enters the basement, violence erupts. Because this environment is essentially white turf, black folk are subject to white invasion at every level. There is no protective cocoon provided for black musicians here. Just in case the audience misses the point, Wilson engages the band members in a discussion of the building itself:

> LEVEE: Nigger, what is you talking about? I'm talking about the room. I ain't talking about no skin and air. I'm talking about something I can see! Last time the band room was upstairs. This time it's downstairs. Next time it be over there. I'm talking about what I can see...

> TOLEDO: Hell, I know what you talking about. I just said everything changing...
>
> LEVEE: That door! Nigger, you see that door?... That door wasn't there before.
>
> CUTLER: Levee, you wouldn't know your right from your left. This is where they used to keep the recording horns and things...and damn if that door wasn't there. How in hell else you gonna get in here? Now, if you talking about they done switched rooms, you right.... (24–25)

The implication is not simply that the black man has no place to rest, but that his place lies at the bottom of life (a note touched again in *The Piano Lesson*). And the door, viewed as entrance or exit, is also under the white man's control. Hence, while the rearrangement of the room is itself a metaphor of change, the limit of one way out or in contributes to a sense of entrapment in the basement, much like "stacking niggers" in the hold of the slave ship as described by Holloway in *Two Trains Running*. Wilson even closes the play with Cutler asking Slow Drag to get Mr. Irvin down to the basement to deal with Levee's murder of Toledo. In the twenties, black music, a *lieu de mémoire* for the African American and a reminder of his unique identity, is simply a money-producing commodity for the white man.

In *Ma Rainey*, August Wilson presents the essential dilemma facing African Americans in particular and all American immigrants in general. How much should a person retain of his past "old country" heritage and how much should he adapt to the "new" American world? If the blues links African Americans with the African and Southern "life world" and its survival insures a sense of specific identity and value for the black man, won't its rearrangement to suit white needs result in a continuing loss of self-worth in the relinquishment of the black man's personal property?

> The question we've been wrestling with since the emancipation Proclamation is "What are we going to do? Do we assimilate into American society and thereby lose our culture, or do we maintain our culture separate from the dominant cultural values and participate in the American society rather than as blacks who have adopted European values?" And I think that this is a question that, for the past hundred years, black America has been trying to figure out and debating which way should we go.[9]

Toledo pinpoints the problem with this kind of cultural accommodation:

> As long as the colored man look to white folks to put the crown on what he say...as long as he looks to white folks for approval...then he ain't never gonna find out who he is and what he's about. He's just gonna be about what white folks want him to be about. That's one sure thing. (37)

---

[9]   August Wilson cited in Shannon, 213.

However, the solution is not a simple one because of divisiveness within the black group itself. The African American odyssey in America is beset with ruptures of all kinds which inhibit the much-needed formation of a sense of community, a situation of which both Toledo and Wilson are acutely aware:

> What you think...I'm gonna solve the colored man's problems by myself? I said, we. You understand that? We. That's every living colored man in the world got to do his share. Got to do his part. I ain't talking about what I'm gonna do...or what you or Cutler or Slow Drag or anybody else. I'm talking about all of us together. What all of us is gonna do. That's what I'm talking about, nigger! (42)

Disagreement finds expression in the constant comparison between city and country behavior, North and South, Africa and America, dress and music, as well as Christian and African religion. Ma Rainey's "old jug band music" collides, like two trains on the same track, with Levee's urban dance arrangements and the new songs he's writing for Sturdyvant. In much the same way Toledo's recognition of Slow Drag's African mode of naming shared experiences (another *lieu de mémoire*) to get a bit of Cutler's reefer, provokes Slow Drag and Levee's denial of their African past.

> LEVEE: You don't see me running around in no jungle with no bone between my nose .
> SLOW DRAG: Nigger, I ain't no African! I ain't doing no African nothing! (32)

After denying this "bond of kinship," Levee ridicules both the African American history of Blacks as slaves/farmers in the South and the importance of education. He calls Toledo's shoes "clodhoppers you can't dance in," and facetiously denigrates Toledo as another Booker T. Washington "making the lot of the colored man better for him here in America." On the other hand, Toledo worries about Levee selling his soul to the devil by accommodating his music to the white man, much like the murderer Eliza Cotter who served and dressed like the carpetbaggers during Reconstruction. When Irvin steps in the bandroom and insists that they rehearse Levee's rendition, Levee crows:

> Hell, the man's the one putting out the record! He gonna put out what he wanna put out!... Who's the boss: Ma's the boss on the road! We at a recording session. Mr. Sturdyvant and Mr. Irvin say what's gonna be here! We's in Chicago, we ain't in Memphis.... (37–38)

Unfortunately, Levee's later betrayal by a white man will provoke the play's tragic conclusion.

Wilson continues his analysis of black/white power dynamics in his delegation of the dramatic action to one of the three levels of the set. Irvin summons the black men in the basement to collect sandwiches in the studio. When Sturdyvant joins Irvin in the studio, he complains of Ma's lateness with the implication that she's operating on Colored People's Time and treating them with disrespect. Sturdyvant exits back up to the control booth before Ma, dressed in furs like the Blues star she is, arrives at the studio with her lover Dussie Mae and her Arkansas country-boy nephew in tow. Yet even her "star" status doesn't prevent her from being arrested for assault and battery by the policeman who enters with her! A ruckus ensues and Sturdyvant enters from the control booth only to be told by Ma Rainey to get away from her. "That's the last thing I need...to go through some of your shit!" (51). Sturdyvant disappears back into the control booth and Irvin takes over by bribing the policeman who's satisfied "as long as someone is responsible for them" (52). Wilson sets the 1927 social context of racial prejudice on the part of Chicago cab drivers, police, and producers who refuse to provide heat or cokes for the talent. White men perceive black people as incapable of taking care of themselves, a holdover from slavery. What we discover here is that the studio level where white and black interact is as contentious as the basement level where the black musicians argue with each other.

After Irvin tells Toledo to take the sandwiches down to the bandroom, we return to the black men talking about themselves. In a series of shared anecdotes, Wilson's characters present African American history to the audience and to each other and try to deal with the perceived *status quo* describing the black man as a "leftover from history" (57). Toledo says:

> Everybody come from different places in Africa, right? Come from different tribes and things. Soon awhile they began to make one big stew. (57)

Wilson tells us about African American history through stories of eyewitnesses. A seemingly casual reference to Slow Drag's grandparents tossing nuts in the stew not only testifies to African roots, but also increases the audience's awareness that the slave trade and the Great Diaspora of black peoples did not occur far back in time whether viewed from the perspective of the characters in 1927 or today's audience.

Wilson pinpoints the notion that the white man wants to dump slavery's leftovers unless he can continue to make money from the black man. Commodifying black music is the white man's *modus operandi* in this play. In contrast, Wilson heroicizes Ma Rainey through her insistence on singing her own song, called "old circus bullshit" by Levee (64), and on a stuttering Sylvester doing the traditional introduction. Ultimately, Ma goes down to the band room and gets her way despite opposition from both blacks and whites. Not only does she pass the music through her own family line, but she ultimately relieves Sylvester from stuttering. Again, the music becomes a metaphor for a black man finding his own voice. After Ma leaves, Sturdyvant for the first time enters the band room and exploits Levee's disappointment by asking for his original dance music, "You can shake it..." (66). When the other band members razz Levee for "shuffling them feet" (67) and being "spooked up with the white men" (67) like the old slaves, Levee defends himself in true "warrior spirit" fashion:

> I can say yessir to whoever I please....
>   Levee got to be Levee! And he don't need nobody messing with him about the white man—cause you don't know nothing about me. (68)

Once again Wilson gives voice to African American history through an eyewitness character. Through the story of his family, Levee defies the other band members:

> We was living in Jefferson County, about eighty miles outside of Natchez. My daddy's name was Memphis...Memphis Lee Green...had him near fifty acres of good farming land. I'm talking about good land! Grow anything you want! He done gone off of shares and bought this land from Mr. Hallie's widow woman after he done passed on. Folks called him an uppity nigger cause he done saved and borrowed to where he could buy this land and be independent. (69)

Just as Levee's father was criticized for moving up from sharecropper to landowner, the other band members criticize Levee for trying to please whites with his musical version. Wilson draws a parallel between Levee's situation and his family's story. He uses Levee's description of his mother's gang-rape, his father's first smiling at the same crackers who attacked his mother, selling his land and then killing half of them, only to be lynched and set on fire in the end. Levee, left bleeding to death, witnessed the event and was saved by a black midwife after the white doctor refused to see him. Ironically, Levee does not perceive the moral of his own story. For Wilson, success comes from the black community and not from reliance on the white man, who at the top level of the setting's architectural hierarchy, still governs from the control booth. Act One ends in the bandroom with a wish to end white oppression expressed in Slow Drag's song: "If I had my say I would tear this old building down" (71).

Now that the major conflict has been set up in Act One, Wilson proceeds to illustrate how a lone levee (Levee) couldn't possibly dam up the flow of the Mississippi (Ma) or quickly take over the power of the white man. We return to the meeting ground of the recording studio to hear Ma staking out her claim to sing her song the way she wants to, despite Sturdyvant trying to tell her how to sing it from the control booth. Ma insists that Sylvester do the introduction because "This is what's gonna help him" (78). Demanding her Coca-Cola, she calls the situation as she sees it: "If you colored and can make them some money, then you alright with them. Otherwise, you just a dog in the alley" (79). At the same time in the band room, Levee is excited about giving his music to Sturdyvant and voices his dream of his own band to Dussie Mae. In the white market economy, Levee and many others want a piece of the pie and are willing to accommodate themselves to achieve that goal. Unfortunately, he relies on Sturdyvant to get his new band and his music produced. Back up in the recording studio, Irvin unjustly blames Levee for the recording failure when his own poor maintenance is the cause.

Wilson understands black frustration about being at the bottom of the economic barrel beyond the bandroom. He lets us know that the band members' families work at jobs running elevators in St. Louis or farming in Plattsville. An ambitious Levee describes the current situation:

> Niggers got a right to be dissatisfied. Is you gonna be satisfied with a bone somebody done throwed you when you see them eating the whole hog?...
> You satisfied sitting in one place. You got to move on down the road from where you sitting...and all the time you got to keep an eye out for that devil who's looking to buy up souls. And hope you get lucky and find him! (93–94)

This comment incenses Cutler who calls this blasphemy, but Toledo tells Cutler they're "imitation white men" (94) who "sold Africa for the price of tomatoes" (94). Levee refuses to accept the label, but relies on Sturdyvant and Irvin to produce his music, get his band together, and make the records. He doesn't recognize that the colored folks made Ma a star, not the white folks. Trying to get respect from the white folk doesn't really work—even Ma can't stay in a white hotel or get into a Chicago cab.

For Wilson, the black man selling out to the white man is not just an economic, but a spiritual dilemma. He sees that Christianity, while declaring all men equal in the sight of God, can be a tool for the white man to keep the black man down. Contextualizing Cutler's story of whites hassling the Reverend Gates in the African-style ritualistic naming of all the towns from Tallahassee to Atlanta along the railroad line, a *lieu de mémoire* of the northward migration, illustrates his point. White folks don't respect the Bible-toting colored minister and use their guns to make him dance. Levee, remembering his mother's plea to Jesus when she was attacked, believes God fails to act because He's the "white man's God" (98). Cutler attacks Levee with a knife, but doesn't follow through when Levee focuses on defying God

Himself (an action later taken by Troy in *Fences*). Wilson has set the path for frustration to lead to violence within the black community.

Before things settle down, Wilson moves the band back to the studio where Irvin, over the speaker in the control booth, congratulates the musicians in the possessive voice of the new owner: "We have that, boys.... We've got ourselves some winners" (100). The white man still doesn't want to pay the black man. Ma, however, retains her own independence. She fires Levee for making the session difficult and trying to alter her songs. She also refuses to satisfy Irvin, entering from the control booth to the studio, who demands she pay Sylvester out of her own fee. Even Cutler demands cash, because no one will honor checks from a black man. While Ma recognizes her own worth as expressed in her music and the legal power of ownership until she signs the release, back in the bandroom the men are waiting to be paid. Only after Ma signs the release do both white men enter the band room for the first time to pay the men. When Irvin goes off to let the black men out, Sturdyvant lags behind to exploit Levee by giving him five dollars apiece for his songs and kills any hopes of recording or starting his own band. The sense of "we told you so" reverberates in the room as the other musicians silently pack up. Toledo's stepping on Levee's shoe, the symbol of his urban emancipation and success, exacerbates his humiliation. Levee retaliates out of his increasing rage at Sturdyvant by knifing Toledo in the back. The violence of this misplaced attack affects one of his own black brothers and not the source, the exploitative white man.

Like Hellman, Wilson sees the denial of self-worth, here encapsulated in blues music, as a primary cause of aimless violence. To explore the causes of insecurity and build a sense of community for African Americans, he will no longer employ a white setting for the rest of his plays. From now on he will move from black houses (the Maxsons', Charles and Vera's, Louise and Hedley's) to black businesses (Holly's boardinghouse, Becker's jitney station, Memphis's diner) — all located in the Hill District of Pittsburgh. By releasing the voices of his characters within the safe environment of a black neighborhood, Wilson will make sure that no white man will directly hinder the African American's search for identity and a home in America.

Fences

> ROSE: Times have changed since you was playing baseball, Troy. That was before the war. Times have changed a lot since then. They got lots of colored boys playing ball now. Baseball and football.[10]

---

[10]   August Wilson, *Fences*, 9.

In *Fences*, Wilson creates a "private enclave" in the all-black Hill District neighborhood—a secure cocooning environment free from white invasion which allows for open discussion among the inhabitants which they and the audience are both meant to hear. Here we are on black turf, not the controlling white environment of *Ma Rainey's Black Bottom*.

On this unifying and familiar base, he chooses certain "moments of history" or times of change in his ongoing examination of the history of African Americans in America. *Fences* houses *lieux de mémoire* on several levels: the music (as in *Ma Rainey*), the development of professional sports, job expansion to include union membership and the military; and the setting of the Maxson house and yard which presents the new situation of post-World War II property ownership available to blacks.

In the play's preface, Wilson delineates the breach, the disjunction between America's promise of post-Abolition freedom and the actual opportunities open to blacks and foregrounds his real subject within the following context. He writes:

> Near the turn of the century, the destitute of Europe sprang on the city with tenacious claws and an honest and solid dream.... The city grew. It nourished itself and offered each man a partnership limited only by his talent, his guile, and his willingness and capacity for hard work. For the immigrants of Europe, a dream dared and won true....
>
> The descendants of African slaves were offered no such welcome or participation. (xvii)

Wilson notes the massive migration northward by blacks on foot and by rail in search of freedom and jobs promised by the American Dream, only to meet with resistance. He writes of black origins in the South, using the geographic place names, so important to Melvin Dixon's notion of *lieux de mémoire*:

> They came from places called the Carolinas and the Virginias, Georgia, Alabama, Mississippi and Tennessee. They came strong, eager, searching. The city rejected them, and they fled and settled along the riverbanks and under bridges in shallow, ramshackle houses made of sticks and tar-paper. They collected rags and wood. They sold the use of their muscles and their bodies. They cleaned houses and washed clothes, they shined shoes, and in quiet desperation and vengeful pride, they stole and lived in pursuit of their own dream: That they could breathe free, finally, and stand to meet life with the force of dignity and whatever eloquence the heart could call upon. (xvii)

Given this unreceptive urban context, Wilson asks us to examine the position of black Americans in 1957. He recognizes the solidification of the "industrial might of America" (xvii), the winning of World War II using "loyalty and patriotism as its fuel" (xvii), postwar prosperity, and the success of the Milwaukee Braves in the World Series. So where does the black man stand in pursuit of the American dream in a period before the turbulent decade of the Sixties with its explosion in the Civil Rights movement and Black Power? Following World War II, probably the most disruptive event of the twentieth century, African Americans would find new access to professional baseball once Jackie Robinson broke the color barrier in 1947, union membership with positions in the trades previously reserved for whites, disability pensions from the government for veterans and funding from the GI Bill allowing for further educational opportunity and assistance toward property ownership.

Wilson crystallizes change in the sports arena through Cory and Troy's argument about black participation in the professional baseball leagues in Act One: Scene Three. John Timpane in "Filling the Time: Reading History in the Drama of August Wilson" contends, "baseball operates metonymically, as a metaphoric stand-in for the troubled changes of 1957."[11] Despite Cory's citing future World Series champions like the Braves' Hank Aaron and Wes Covington among others, Troy clings to his prewar experience of racial discrimination. Even Rose's mention of Jackie Robinson can do nothing to change Troy's mind. His is a losing attitude, much like that of the Anatolian Troy destined to lose the battle to ancient Greece. Not until 1959 would every major league team have a black player in the piecemeal process of integration. Troy's bitterness over his own exclusion from professional baseball prevents him from seeing his son's opportunity for further education represented by the college football recruiter from North Carolina who pursues Cory.

> I told that boy about that football stuff. The white man ain't gonna let him get nowhere with that football.... He ought to go and get recruited in how to fix cars or something where he can make a living. (8)

Despite the fact that Troy is illiterate, doesn't possess a driver's license and gets opposition from another black garbage collector Brownie, Troy still wins union promotion to the white man's level as truck driver. Troy's own advancement does not prevent him from urging Cory to stick with his job at the A&P and get a trade. Ultimately, Cory, like many minority young men, turns to the U.S. military to advance in the world. He becomes a living icon in his Marine uniform when he appears for his father's funeral in the final

---

11 John Timpane, "Filling the Time: Reading History in the Drama of August Wilson," in Alan Nadel, *May All Your Fences Have Gates: Essays on the Drama of August Wilson* (Iowa City: U of Iowa P, 1994), 70.

scene. Even Lyons, doing time for forgery in the workhouse, tells him to "stick with Uncle Sam and retire early" (94).

In addition to sports, music was another route for Blacks towards recognizable success in America. Whereas Wilson made the blues singer Ma Rainey a kind of living *lieu de mémoire* in *Ma Rainey's Black Bottom*, here music again serves as a conduit of black culture and provides a own sense of identity:

> I know I got to eat. But I got to live too. I need something that gonna help me to get out of the bed in the morning. Make me feel like I belong in the world. I don't bother nobody. I just stay with my music cause that's the only way I can find to live in the world Otherwise there ain't no telling what I might do. (18)

Wilson goes on to ground and give significance to Lyons' efforts when Bono tries to get Troy to hear his son play at the Crawford Grill, an actual place known for good music, the home of Billy Eckstine.

Wilson's far-ranging musical elements in *Fences* cite disruptive moments in black history. He alludes to Lyons' African roots exemplified in his title of "King of the Jungle" (48). He notes Troy's ex-slave, later sharecropper father's Old Blue Song with its allusions to tracking runaway slaves like possums and the chains and shovels used by blacks impressed into road work gangs like Joe Turner's. Here, however, Troy's father puts his effort into sending true Blue to the Promised Land, not to death and capture by the white man. While the song of Old Blue belongs to Troy's father, its completion in Raynell and Cory's duet finally allows Cory to reconcile with the spirit of his dead father "treeing possums in the Promised Land" (99) and fulfills Wilson's declared intention in the prefatory poem to forgive the sins of the fathers.

> When the sins of our fathers visit us
> We do not have to play host.
> We can banish them with forgiveness
> As God, in His Largeness and Laws.

Wilson also refers to the Second Diaspora in Troy's railroad song. He uses it as a lullaby for his as yet unnamed baby girl by that Florida gal Alberta and as a plea to Rose to "give her a ride" by taking her in as her own daughter. Yet Wilson never allows Gabe, his "spectacle" character, to give Troy an archangel's sendoff by successfully blowing his trumpet to open the gates of heaven at the play's close. Instead Wilson provides an African, not a Christian solution. Paralleling Sylvester's overcoming his stutter with the "tent intro" to Ma Rainey's song, Gabe's howl at his inability to play culminates in his ritualistic, atavistic dance on the dirt, a brother's celebration of a spirit uniting with those of the ancestors. For Wilson, music serves to combine history, religion, and the quest for identity into a single, yet complex *lieu de mémoire*.

Gabe becomes a "spectacle" character pinpointing economic change for the black man in postwar America as well. Gabriel becomes a way out for a man who works hard, but didn't "have a pot to piss in."

> That's the only way I got a roof over my head...cause of that metal plate. If my brother didn't have that metal plate in his head...I wouldn't have a pot to piss in or a window to throw it out of. (28)

Initially the audience supports Troy's use of Gabe's disability money because they understand his story. Troy's personal history echoes similar stories of migrating blacks. Troy had walked two hundred miles to Mobile from the 42 acres of Mr. Lubin's land his daddy sharecropped to support 11 kids and sought freedom in Pittsburgh. He couldn't get a job, lived under a bridge, robbed for food, met Lyons' mother and got her pregnant, killed a man in a robbery attempt, ended up in the penitentiary for 15 years (where he met Bono and learned to play baseball) and sat out the draft (51–53). Gabriel's disability pay as a war veteran allows Troy to buy his house and purchase furniture on credit. We see a man who refuses to buy a television for Cory because the roof needs tarring, and faithfully hands over his weekly paycheck to Rose. Troy, however, defends his brother's need for freedom when it serves his own purposes:

> Don't nobody wanna be locked up, Rose. What you wanna lock him up for? Man go over there and fight the war...messing around with them Japs, get half his head blown off...and they give him a lousy three thousand dollars. And I had to swoop down on that. (28)
>
> ....
>
> The man done had his life ruined fighting for what? And they wanna take and lock him up. Let him be free. He don't bother nobody. (65)

Gabe, however, upsets Troy's plans when he decides to be independent by selling vegetables from the Strip and renting a room from Pearl with his government pay. Troy resists Rose's suggestion that Gabe go to the veterans' hospital even after he pays the police fine for Gabe's disturbing the peace. Yet when Troy needs additional funds to support his affair with Alberta, he betrays his brother and commits him. Ultimately, Troy denies Gabe the very freedom he's earned. Ironically, just as the plantation owners bought and sold slaves, Troy enslaves his own brother to get what he wants. For Wilson, money for a refrigerator or a television is peanuts compared to the sale of a human life.

In Wilson's world, jobs—as proof of worth and independence—are immensely important, but responsibility to one's family is paramount. He ranks the honest labor of garbage-collecting and the trades above gambling, and criticizes Pope for serving white men meat in the stew in his numbers-won restaurant. Yet nothing is as inhumane or irresponsible as brother betraying brother or husband betraying wife. Fragmentation of the black family, as perceived by Rose in her comment that "My whole family is half" (68), is not only the result of human frailty, but also of slavery's legacy, "searching out the New Land" (50), the residual bitterness from racial discrimination in sports and continuing economic restrictions in the "land of opportunity." While the Maxsons are the focus here, Wilson's overriding concern is binding up the black community itself. For him, the community is an extended family.

While assorted Pittsburgh place names, such as the Logan Street boardinghouse where Bono and Lucille first live when they come to the city and folkloric references such as Uncle Remus and Aunt Jemimah, all add to a sense of history both geographic and anecdotal, the stage setting provides an even more powerful three-dimensional *lieu de mémoire* and frames the family tragedy. In 1957, a black family can live in its own house, albeit in an older, poorer section of the city. The "ancient two-story brick house" owned by the Maxsons may be shabby and in need of repair, but it provides a porch with chairs of dubious value and an old-fashioned icebox and a yard which enables neighbors to visit. While the house, probably from the early part of the nineteenth century like others in the Hill District, would once have belonged to white folks, now it belongs to black owners. Property has now come to those once considered property themselves.

Wilson emphasizes the small dirt yard with its partially built fence, an object promised to his wife Rose. It is important that the yard remains open to the community until Troy betrays his family and takes the bat to his own son. In the context of the play, the baseball bat leaning against the tree from which hangs a ball made of rags addresses the rags to riches path to freedom for blacks in sports. It also visually represents Troy's dreams and the collision of his ideas with those of his son. Perhaps most important of all is the metaphorical exploration of space which links the dirt yard outside with the spiritual world of Life and Death—a world larger than the individual inside a room within his own home, a boardinghouse, a diner or even a recording studio belonging to the white man. There is something elemental here—whether it be the location for discussions of fatherhood, family conflict, or a confrontation with Death itself. The yard, too, is the location for Raynell's garden, the place for growth, hope and reconciliation as well as the scene of

Gabe's celebratory ritualistic dance at the play's close. The earth itself provides a home for the black man's journey from Africa to America, from the farm to the city, from barbecue to voodoo. The fence may exclude Cory and Bono temporarily or keep Troy in Rose's vicinity, but the resultant lonely isolation, seen and heard in Troy's drunken version of "Blue" (82, 84), isn't worth the long-lasting hard wood the fence is made of. Without the extended family of the black community, life is not worth living.

It is precisely by building his neighborhood cocoon that Wilson provides his characters with an environment secure from white invasion and a place where the sharing of oral history and the examination of black values in terms of individual identity, community practices, and place in American society can occur. As Troy says to baby Raynell on the porch steps, that shabby bridge between outside and inside—"I been homeless" and sings: "Please, Mr. Engineer let a man ride the line" (79).

Joe Turner's Come and Gone

In *Joe Turner's Come and Gone*, Wilson continues to layer *lieux de mémoire* in his construction of African American history. Just as with *Ma Rainey* and *Fences*, August Wilson has written a Preface presenting the play's historical context, the 1911 city of Pittsburgh pulsating with rapid-fire industrial growth (particularly, steel), and utilizing an enormous labor force building bridges, laying roads, carving tunnels, and constructing houses. All men who flock to the city are imbued with the American Dream of greater opportunity for all who work hard and of rights to freedom and the pursuit of happiness. It is the dream of foreigners, "the destitute of Europe" (*Fences*, xvii), and country folk, both black and white, who wish to make their way in the big city. Hopes are high and the discrepancy between America's promise and practice, so apparent in *Fences*, is not the focus here. Instead the fragmentation of an African American "life world" is. Against the larger environment of a burgeoning northern industrial city, Wilson sets into relief one of the greatest ruptures in the history of African Americans subsequent to the Middle Passage, the practice of Slavery in the South, the eruption of the Civil War, Abolition, and Reconstruction. It is the time of the Second Diaspora when newly-freed blacks emigrated to northern cities in search of jobs and themselves—their families and their traditions shattered by Post-Abolition upheaval in Southern agrarian society that forces blacks, armed only with Bibles and guitars, onto rivers, dirt roads, and railroad lines in search of ways, including jobs, to ensure their survival and validate their worth as free human beings.

No one describes this journey as well as August Wilson:

From the deep and the near South the sons and daughters of newly freed African slaves wander into the city. Isolated, cut off from memory, having forgotten the names of the gods and only guessing at their faces, they arrive dazed and stunned, their hearts kicking in their chest with a song worth singing. They arrive carrying Bibles and guitars, their pockets lined with dust and fresh hope, marked men and women seeking to scrape from the narrow, crooked cobbles and the fiery blasts of the coke furnace a way of bludgeoning and shaping the malleable parts of themselves into a new identity as free men of definite and sincere worth.

....

Foreigners in a strange land, they carry as part and parcel of their baggage a long line of separation and disbursement which informs their sensibilities and marks their conduct as they search for ways to reconnect, to reassemble, to give clear and luminous meaning to the song which is both a wail and a whelp of joy.[12]

As in the plays previously studied, *Joe Turner's Come and Gone* contains *lieux de mémoire* in its music, its mentioned geographic locales from Texas to Tennessee—its manners in dress, food, and modes of expression,[13] its jobs from road building to ironing to playing the blues at Seefus's place, its setting and its heavy emphasis on African traditions still held by descendants of slaves brought from Africa.[14]

As in *Ma Rainey's Black Bottom*, the title of this play is also the name of a real blues song, the lament of black women whose men had been stolen away by Joe Turner, the Tennessee governor's brother, who pressed them into chain gangs and forced labor on abandoned former plantations for periods of at least seven years away from their families during the Reconstruction.[15] While Ma's blues proclaimed her identity and Southern roots in "tent music," W.C. Handy recorded "Joe Turner's Come and Gone," describing the agony of African Americans experiencing the ruthless behavior of an actual historical figure and the resultant destruction of the family structure, already hard hit earlier on slavery's auction block. Because he was kidnapped while trying to convert a group of gamblers and put into one of Joe Turner's chain gangs, Herald Loomis is himself a living "site of memory," a "man who done forgot his song" (71), according to Bynum.

Bynum is Wilson's Binding Man whose job in the play is to "reconnect, reassemble, to give luminous meaning to the song which is both a wail and a whelp of joy" (the preface n.p.). He binds up the wounds of slavery and im-

---

12 August Wilson, *Joe Turner's Come and Gone,* preface, n.p.
13 See Trudier Harris, "August Wilson's Folk Traditions," in Marilyn Elkins, *August Wilson: A Casebook* (New York: Garland Publishing, 1994) and Patricia Gantt, "Ghosts from "Down There": The Southernness of August Wilson," in Marilyn Elkins, *August Wilson: A Casebook* (New York: Garland Publishing, 1994).
14 Shannon, 127–137.
15 Gantt, 74.

pressment and returns the black man to his African past and sense of self. In the play, Bynum confronts Loomis with the Joe Turner song to jolt Loomis into the release of his own voice. Bynum leads Loomis to the discovery of his value as a human being and to the recognition that he is much more than mere physical property doing the work that Joe Turner was capable of doing himself (73). Loomis then connects Bynum with the harrowing, yet beautiful vision of the Middle Passage's "bones on the water" at the end of Act I. He recognizes Bynum as "one of them bones people" (73), metaphorically connected with those Yoruban priests utilizing bones for their predictions and by extension with the Middle Passage and an ancestral history going all the way back to Africa. Just as Bynum had found his own song through his vision of his father and his "Healing Song" on the road, Bynum here meets his own "shiny man" in Loomis whom he helps heal and bind by passing along an ancestral tradition which will culminate in Loomis's self-lacerating ritual of self-sufficiency in Act Two. Because Loomis finally understands his own self worth, he does not need to draw a knife against another black man (Bynum), accept Joe Turner's robbery of black freedom to prop up white power or Martha Pentecost's belief in a white Christ. Loomis will take responsibility for himself and not look to a white God for salvation.

Bynum has an unusual helper in this journey of reassembly and reconnection—a white man. Selig, whose name in German means "holy" or "sacred," is not simply a door-to-door peddler of pots and pans. He is the "People Finder" whose trade route, another *lieu de mémoire*, allows him to meet and reunite black family members scattered northward in the Second Diaspora. Certainly he does his job for a fee, but he is also another living *lieu de mémoire*, the container of the entire history of the white man's relations with the black man in America from slave trading, the capturing of runaway slaves, to the uniting of fragmented black friends, lovers, and families. He tells Loomis:

> I can't promise anything but we been finders in my family for a long time. Bringers and finders. My great-granddaddy used to bring Nigras across the ocean on ships. That wasn't no easy job either. Sometimes the winds would blow so hard you'd think the hand of God was set against the sails. But it set him well in pay and he settled in this new land and found him a wife of good Christian charity with a mind for kids and the like and well...here I am, Rutherford Selig. You're in good hands, mister. Me and my daddy have found plenty Nigras. My daddy, rest his soul, used to find runaway slaves for the plantation bosses. He was the best there was at it. Jonas B. Selig. Had him a reputation stretched clean across the country. After Abraham Lincoln give you all Nigras your freedom papers and with you all looking all over for each other...we started finding Nigras for Nigras. Of course, it don't pay as much. But the People Finding business ain't so bad. (41)

Loomis gives Selig his dollar and Selig takes off upriver, significantly the route with its specific geographic places names delineates another *lieu de mémoire*, one known not only to runaway slaves and migrating Blacks, but also to Bynum:

> You going up around my way. I used to go all up through there. Blawnox...Clairton. Used to go up to Rankin and take that first right-hand road. I wore many a pair of shoes out walking around that way. You'd have thought I was a missionary spreading the gospel the way I wandered all around them parts. (42)

With information gleaned from Seth, Bynum gives Selig geographical clues to the location of Martha Pentecost, Loomis's wife. Wilson also conflates his role as a guide in Loomis's spiritual quest in a combined African and Christian context. The African conjure man and rootworker becomes a missionary trying to save Loomis's soul in conjunction with Selig's search. Significantly, Seth and Selig exit together, despite Bertha's warning that

> This old People Finding business is for the birds. He ain't never found nobody he ain't took away. Herald Loomis, you just wasted your dollar. (42)

Loomis, however, keeps his faith in Selig's ability to find Martha:

> He say he find her. He say he find her by Saturday. I'm gonna wait till Saturday. (42)

Simultaneously, Wilson leaves open the possibility of white assistance (not direction) in the reassembly of an African American community. Taking away and finding brings African American history full circle.

To contrast with the play's wanderers, Wilson introduces the Hollys who have permanently settled in Pittsburgh. Seth Holly is both the son of free Northern blacks (not slaves) and the owner of his own home. Taking advantage of the stream of newly freed slaves wandering northward in search of work and family, Seth rents rooms. Additionally, he works as a metalworker for white man Olowski at night and makes pots and pans for Selig. He dreams of going into business for himself, but he can't get a loan from white moneylenders without putting his house up as collateral. Unlike those who possess nothing but Bibles and guitars, Seth knows the value of owning property in America and prides himself on his urban upbringing as opposed to the country background of the travellers. He is a Christian church-goer who respects Martha Pentecost and won't reveal her whereabouts to a crazy-seeming Loomis. At the same time, he retains some African traditions like the African call and response dance, the juba, every Sunday night as well. His wife Bertha is the heart of the household and the mother of all—providing food (grits, yams and biscuits, fried chicken reminiscent of both the South and Africa), clean bed linens, womanly advice, and a pragmatic practice of Christian and African beliefs—to all who pass through this way station.

Wilson needs a vessel to contain all the characters' stories and ground them in a tangible and credible sense of history. He chooses, therefore, to locate his play in a Pittsburgh boarding house at the height of the Second Diaspora in 1911. As a metaphor for transience, rootlessness, and passing through, the boarding house is an appropriate surrounding for a gathering of those in search of some kind of meaning for their lives. It is not a bulwark being invaded from without as in Hellman's plays, instead it is a protective cocoon for African American characters struggling to find their identity after the debilitating history of slavery and Reconstruction. While the most disturbing character is that of Loomis, the personification of that dark face in Romare Bearden's collage "Mill Hand's Lunch Bucket,"[16] his journey is simply the most severe of the lot. Each has his own tale of broken relationships—Mattie and Jack, Molly and many men, Reuben and Zonia. Each tale is supported with the specificity of what state the characters came from and even what crop they grew or picked. Even the one white character on stage is not a hostile invader, but a carrier and witness to African American history. Wilson incorporates a variety of elements from black experience in his characters' stories—the North and South, city and country, Christian and African religion – and pulls them together to focus on the one basic need underlying these differences: to find again a sense of human worth previously denied in slavery and to establish a new kind of family in the extended black community. If we track the use of the space, we can see that Wilson's setting simply physicalizes and contains the varied journeys of all in the group. The community becomes the family.

Wilson, expanding the metaphorical resonance of house and yard employed in *Fences*, here takes us both inside the house and out to the yard. The house itself is divided into a parlor and kitchen and stairs leading to the boarders' rooms upstairs. Seth and Bertha live off the kitchen which in turn leads outside to the outhouse, Seth's tinsmithing workshed and yard including a garden. Guests arrive through the front door, go through the parlor and then upstairs or to the kitchen.

Individual soul-searching occurs primarily within the interior of the house while the outside space reminds us of the larger world of life and death. Significantly, the heart of the household lies in the kitchen where peo-

---

16   Shannon, 123; Joan Fishman, "Romare Bearden, August Wilson, and the Traditions of African Performance," in Nadel, 134–37.

ple gather to eat, to gossip, and to juba. It is the scene of intimate, personal activity where we hear most of the private stories of the wayfarers. The yard, as in *Fences*, is the territory of new life with its garden and environment for children. Additionally it is the place of the spiritual—whether it be Bynum's bloodletting ritual with the pigeons, the wind-announced appearance of Miss Mabel's ghost, or the love scene between Zonia and Reuben. Wilson will employ the same technique later on in *Seven Guitars*.

When Wilson wants to make an event more public and more significant for the characters onstage and for the audience as well, the action expands from the kitchen to include the yard or the parlor. At the heart of the house lies Bertha's kitchen where all but two of the play's nine scenes originate—II, 2 where Seth and Bynum play dominoes in the parlor and Bynum confronts Loomis with the Joe Turner song and the story of the vision of his father and II, 4 where Reuben tells Zonia about the ghost of Seth's dead mother Miss Mabel forcing him to release his dead friend Eugene's pigeons and ultimately makes her his "girl" by kissing her. One typical device is to have characters in the kitchen observe and comment on something outside, such as Seth belittling Bynum's circling ritual with the pigeon blood as "mumbo jumbo" despite Bertha's protest to the contrary. In this way, Wilson frames the simultaneous and schizophrenic presence of both African religion and white Christianity within the black community. At the end of Act I, all the residents, except Loomis, participate in the rousing juba that reaches a near frenzy when Herald bursts into the house through the front door and angrily tries, defying the Holy Ghost, to break up the festivity. When he attempts to escape through the front door, his own vision of bones walking on the water and amassing black flesh throws him to the floor. When breath of life, the holy spirit, begins to rise in him, Loomis attempts to rise and join the men "shaking hands and saying good-bye to each other and walking every whichaway down the road while the ground's starting to shake" and "the world's busting half in two," but he collapses with the effort (55). Despite Bynum's coaching, Herald is too damaged by Joe Turner and white Christianity's emphasis on this life as a vale of tears. Loomis is still too weak to stand up because he can not reconcile the two and still does not know who he is as an African American individual. Wilson here brings all the past horror of the Middle Passage into the present tense and by doing so, makes those onstage and in the audience aware of slavery's human cost to blacks and the enormous strength yet to be found to establish real self-worth and independence.

Wilson's solution to Loomis's dilemma finds its reflection in his physical use of the setting. Wilson builds a compassionate platform for Loomis' epiphany. In Act II, i, Wilson again returns to the kitchen where Seth and Bertha argue about kicking Loomis out of the house, yet admit Bynum's calming influence. Molly enters and declares "It [Loomis's violent fit] don't bother me none. I done seen that kind of stuff before" (58). Just as in the first scene of the play, the couple onstage turn again to Bynum who enters singing his song: "Soon my work will all be done/ I'm going to see the king" (58). Despite Molly's judgment of him as one of those "voodoo people" (60), Bynum has realized that Loomis is his "shiny man" (6) and he's going to heal him and bind his soul together. He goes after Loomis in the next scene by using the Joe Turner song to provoke Loomis to tell his story and help him find his "starting place in the world" (72). It's a starting place he's got to find within himself and not rely on his long lost wife. Wilson uses both parlor and kitchen for this major scene. Next the playwright moves to the intimacy of the kitchen where Bynum gives Mattie her packet of herbs. Bertha advises her about men (Jeremy) and then drags Seth away from Loomis to prevent another confrontation. Left alone with Mattie, Loomis makes his small overture towards this "full woman" (77), only to find out he's even forgotten how to touch, something the two children discover in the following kiss in the yard.

Loomis has to find in himself the capacity to love again within a black community which can acknowledge his pain. Act II, v returns to the kitchen where Bynum, Loomis, Zonia, Bertha, and Mattie wait for Seth to return from work and Selig to come back from his search. After noticing a moment of tenderness between Loomis and Mattie, Bertha initiates a magical dance of blessing, reminiscent of Bynum's circling dance, which includes Seth, Bynum, and Mattie in its celebratory laughter. This joyfulness splits apart as Selig brings Martha Pentecost back to the boardinghouse to find her daughter and Loomis enters through the front door to meet his wife at last. Martha's tale of sharecropping alone on Henry Thompson's place until he kicked her off the land, waiting five years at her mother's, and then deciding to strike out for herself after killing him in her heart is a heartbreaking one. She couldn't drag him behind her "like a sack of cotton" (90) for the rest of her life. While she, too, has suffered the devastating loss of love and family during Reconstruction, Martha relies on Christianity for a solution. Loomis attacks Bynum with a knife as Martha tries to use the Bible to calm him down. He defies the notion of a white Jesus bleeding for him and instead chooses to slash himself across the chest and accept responsibility for his own place in the world with his own blood. Again Wilson starts with intimate dialogue in the kitchen and expands the action beginning with Bertha's dance to include the entire stage because Loomis's "song of self sufficiency" (93) is meant to be seen and heard by those onstage and in the audience. Signifying and loud talking combine in his masterful utilization of the set itself.

The Piano Lesson

> AW: What should we do with our legacy? What would you do if this was your piano? What is our future? Why do we stay up here and let Boy Willie go back down and get some land, something under his feet?[17]

Just as he did for *Joe Turner's Come and Gone,* playwright Wilson turns once again to a collage by fellow Pittsburgh artist Romare Bearden for inspiration. He uses Bearden's "Piano Lesson" image to express the African American odyssey within American history and explore its relation to the larger notion of the American Dream.

> AW: So I got the idea from the painting that there would be a woman and a little girl in the play. And I thought that the woman would be a character who was trying to acquire a sense of self-worth by denying her past. And I felt that she couldn't do that. She had to confront the past, in the person of her brother, who was going to sweep through the house like a tornado coming from the South, bringing the past with him.[18]

Wilson also returns to Pittsburgh, but the time now is that of the Depression—of "breadlines, widespread unemployment, insufficient housing, and a crippled U.S. economy."[19] Simultaneously, the devastation of the cotton economy in the South catapults blacks northward in a Great Migration.

> Blacks suffered sooner, longer, and more profoundly than whites the disastrous effects of the vast economic dislocation of the 1930s. In the South, the cotton economy was hit so hard that the number of Black tenant farmers and sharecroppers decreased by some two hundred thousand from 1930–1940. Industrial workers North and South were laid off or displaced by whites. By 1932 fifty-six percent of Blacks were unemployed.[20]

Many former white farmers or landowners sold off their acreage and also moved to Northern urban, industrial centers to start new businesses. Sutter's

---

[17] Richard Pettengill, "The Historical Perspective," in Marilyn Elkins, *August Wilson: A Casebook* (New York: Garland Publishing, 1994), 225.

[18] Mervyn Rothstein, "Round Five for the Theatrical Heavyweight," *New York Times,* 15 April 1990, sec. 2, I, 8.

[19] Shannon, 150.

[20] Richard Barksdale and Keneth Kinnamon, "Renaissance and Radicalism: 1915–1945," in *Black Writers of America,* ed. Richard Barksdale and Keneth Kinnamon (New York: Macmillan, 1972), 476.

brother manufactures soda fountain equipment in Chicago and his sons no longer farm. Wining Boy, singer and piano player, asks his older brother Doaker:

> WINING BOY: What about them boys Sutter got? How come they ain't farming that land?
> DOAKER: One of them going to school. He left down there and come North to school. The other one ain't got as much sense as that frying pan over yonder. That is the dumbest white man I ever seen. He'd stand in the river and watch it rise till it drown him.[21]

Doaker concludes that white flight from the South was the intelligent thing to do because "That land ain't worth nothing no more. The smart white man's up here in these cities. He cut the land loose and step back and watch you and the dumb white man argue over it" (36). Hence, 1937 marks a time of enormous rupture both economically and culturally in America as both blacks and whites move northward.

Wilson continues layering *lieux de mémoire* in *The Piano Lesson*—music, travel routes, jobs, African notions of the supernatural, and the set. All of the characters, with the exception of a citified Grace, hail from Mississippi. Their overland routes and changing jobs give testimony to the Great Migration and economic hardship in the South. Boy Willie and Lymon Jackson drive 1800 miles from Mississippi to Pittsburgh, despite breakdowns in West Virginia and Sunflower (2–4). Prior to the trip north, both tried to help Berniece's husband Crawley "keep the wolf from the door" by stealing Jim Miller's wood. However, the sheriff caught them in the attempt and murdered Crawley. Lymon and Boy Willie ended up at Parchman Farm prison, a fate shared by Wining Boy and other southern blacks whose labor thereby became free to the white man. Significantly, Boy Willie leads Doaker, Lymon, and Wining Boy in a railroad work song "Oh Lord Berta Berta" that reflects their shared prison experience, yet turns into a juba. They're free men now, hiding out from the sheriff and Stovall's demand for hard labor. After hauling and cutting wood on his cousin's acreage in Stoner County, Lymon purchased Henry Porter's truck for $120 so he had an undetected place to sleep and eventually escape to the North where he plans to work, albeit not too hard, at unloading boxcars. Boy Willie bought the watermelons from old man Pitterford for ten dollars to sell in the North (7) and thereby earn part of the purchase price of land owned by Sutter, who had once owned his family. He plans to change the past by getting his own farm:

---

[21]   August Wilson, *The Piano Lesson,* 29.

That's why I come up here. Sell them watermelons. Get Berniece to sell that piano. Put the two parts with the part I done saved. Walk in there. Tip my hat. Lay my money down on the table. Get my deed and walk on out. This time I get to keep all the cotton. Hire me some men to work it for me. Gin my cotton. Get my seed. And I'll see you again next year. Might even plant some tobacco or some oats. (10)

Boy Willie's looking for another form of self-sufficiency in taking over land being sold off by departing whites—in this case, his family's former slave-owner Sutter. His is the American Dream of the family farm, of owning a piece of land himself, of becoming a free citizen. So despite the fact that Doaker is aware of poor land in the South and we (and August Wilson) know the tragic dustbowl stories of the Thirties so well-conveyed by John Steinbeck in *The Grapes of Wrath*, Boy Willie wants to work hard with the only skills he and his father shared—the manual capability of farming.

What I want to bringa child into this world for? Why I wanna bring somebody else into all this for? I'll tell you this.... If I was Rockefeller I'd have forty or fifty. I'd make one every day. Cause they gonna start out in life with all the advantages. I ain't got no advantages to offer nobody. Many is the time I looked at my daddy and seen him staring off at his hands. I got a little older I know what he was thinking. He sitting there saying, "I got these big old hands but what I'm gonna do with them? Best I can do is make a fifty-acre crop for Mr. Stovall. Got these big old hands capable of doing anything. I can take and build something with these hands. But where's the tools? All I got is these hands. Unless I go out here and kill me somebody and take what they got...it's a long row to hoe for me to get something of my own. So what I'm gonna do with these big old hands? What would you do?"
....
See now...if he had his own land he wouldn't have felt that way. If he had something under his feet that belonged to him he could stand up taller. That's what I'm talking about. Hell, the land is there for everybody. All you got to do is figure out how to get you a piece. Ain't no mystery to life. You just got to go out and meet it square on. If you got a piece of land you'll find everything else fall right into place. You can stand right up next to the white man and talk about the price of cotton...the weather, and anything else you want to talk about. If you teach that girl that she living at the bottom of life, she's gonna grow up and hate you. (91–92)

The difference between Boy Willie and his father lies in Boy Willie's belief that he can buy and work his own farm. For his father, sharecropping seems to be the only option. Hence, Boy Willie practices what he preaches. He does not believe he has to stay at "the bottom of life," but can become his own boss and hold his head high like any other American.

Wining Boy, another of Wilson's travelling musicians, goes back and forth between the North and the South. A piano player, he's made records (like Ma Rainey and Floyd Barton), but this "rambling, gambling man" now has little money, sponges food and drink off Doaker and Berniece, and even goes so far as Arkansas to work for Joe Herrin at fifty cents a day. Searching for a new land like Bono's father and Lyons, Wining Boy left his wife Cleotha behind in the South. His cousin Rupert Bates gives Willa Bryant his address and he reads her letter describing Cleotha's death. He's just one more example, along with Berniece, of the fragmentation of African American families, but he still communicates with those he knows in the South, and he knows everybody including Patchneck Red (John D. from around Tyler) and Lymon's parents.

Most importantly in this play, Wining Boy bears witness to the actual existence of the ghosts of the Yellow Dog, his brother Boy Charles and the four other men burned alive in the boxcar for stealing the piano. He testifies:

> WINING BOY: Nineteen thirty. July of nineteen thirty I stood right there on that spot. It didn't look like nothing was going right in my life. I said everything can't go wrong all the time...let me go down there and call on the Ghosts of the Yellow Dog, see if they can help me. I went down there and right there where them two railroads (the Southern and the Yellow Dog) cross each other...I stood right there on that spot and called out their names. They talk back to you, too. (34–35)

Boy Willie, Doaker, and Wining Boy describe the ghosts' retaliation against a specific list of white men killed—Sutter, Ed Saunders, Howard Peterson, Charlie Webb, Robert Smith of the "nine or ten, eleven or twelve" (34), thereby giving the ghosts a bit of credible reality and preparing the audience for Sutter's spectral visits in the Charles Pittsburgh house. For Wilson spirits are real beings, not just bits of folklore.

As the men discuss the railroad crossing, the audience begins to get a sense of the importance of railroad lines in 1937. In this context Doaker, a Pullman cook and Berniece's uncle, becomes a living *lieu de mémoire* who bears witness to the Great Migration of African Americans:

> DOAKER: Twenty-seven years. Now, I'll tell you something about the railroad. What I done learned after twenty-seven years. See, you got North. You got West. You look over here you got South. Over there you got East. Now you can start from anywhere.... Now, why people going? Their sister's sick. They leaving before they kill somebody...and they sitting across from somebody who's leaving to keep from getting killed. They leaving cause they can't get satisfied. They going to meet someone. I wish I had a dollar for every time that someone wasn't at the station to meet them. I done seen that a lot. In between the time they sent the telegram and the time the person get there...they done forgot all about them.
>
> They got so many trains out there they have a hard time keeping them from running into each other. Got trains going every which away. Got people on all of them. Somebody going where somebody just left. If everybody stay in one place I believe this would be a better world. Now what I done learned after twenty-seven years of railroading is this...if the train stays on the track...it's going to get where

it's going. It might not be where you going. If it ain't, then all you got to do is sit
and wait cause the train's coming back to get you. The train don't never stop. It'll
come back every time. Now I'll tell you another thing.... (18–19)

Like the African *griot*, Doaker testifies to his people's needs and that all-
American condition of mobility, reaching back to the Middle Passage and
emigration in general. Doaker opens Act Two with the railroad song "Gonna
leave Jackson Mississippi," providing a complete list of all the stops along
the way (55-56). It is natural that he will again assume the story-telling role
later in describing the history, supplemented by Boy Willie, of the piano. He
and Boy Willie also provide details about food—chicken, cornbread, greens
and black-eyed peas. Doaker too shares in the family breakup typical of the
African American diaspora. His wife Coreen lives in New York City. In
Pittsburgh, he lives with his niece Berniece and her daughter Maretha. When
"home" in the South, he stays at Jack Slattery's place.

The four remaining characters are all full-time residents of Pittsburgh.
Berniece, Doaker's niece and Crawley's widow, works as a housecleaner for
the white folks in Squirrel Hill. She sends her daughter to another actual locale, the Irene Kaufman Settlement House, to further Maretha's education
towards a better future as a teacher. Avery, who had picked cotton on the
Willshaw place in Mississippi, operates an elevator, its cables made of Pittsburgh steel, in the Gulf building. Setting himself up as a Christian preacher,
he tries to borrow money (not easy for blacks at the time, though not as hard
as it was for the Hollys) to build his own church. Grace, who hustles both
Boy Willie and the womanizing Lymon, functions both to draw attention to
their country ways (73) in contrast to the city's "high life" and to provide
outside witness to Sutter's ghost.

The groundplan of the Charles house is identical to that of *Joe Turner*,
yet it is utilized in a completely different fashion. We have the same kitchen
and parlor downstairs with Doaker's room prominent and opening onto the
kitchen like Seth and Bertha Holly's bedroom. Berniece and Maretha, like
the boardinghouse guests, live upstairs. Unlike the home-like quality of the
Hollys, here we see a "house that is sparsely furnished, and although there is
evidence of a woman's touch, there is a lack of warmth and vigor."[22] Life is
at bay. Wilson lets us know in his very choice of phrase that this will be the
house of a woman who has withdrawn from life. The author makes another
decisive shift from the settings of *Fences* and *Joe Turner* in that there is no
outside yard, no earth, just the vertical structure of the house itself. The dirt
yard only exists in Boy Willie's dream of a farm of his own. The staircase

---

22   August Wilson, *The Piano Lesson*, Preface: the Setting.

ascends to Berniece and Maretha's bedrooms and even further up to the habitat of Sutter's ghost. As in *Ma Rainey's Black Bottom*, the control booth is still at the top of the architecture. The white man, albeit a ghost, still reigns above and occasionally frightens the house's inhabitants by tinkling the keys of the piano.

For the first time in one of his plays, Wilson chooses a physical object, a piece of property, to focus his examination of legacy—both cultural and economic—and expose extant schisms within the black community itself. Dominating the parlor is an old upright piano. On the legs of the piano, carved in the manner of African sculpture, are mask-like figures resembling totems. The carvings are rendered with a grace and power of invention that lifts them out of the realm of craftsmanship and into the realm of art. The piano sits in the center of the Pittsburgh house where Doaker Charles, his niece Berniece, and her daughter Maretha (an African name) all live. It is also the focal point of the conflict between Berniece, who regards it as a relic of family history (the past), and Boy Willie, who looks at it as a source of money, if sold to the white man, to buy Sutter's farm (the future).

Combining art and history, the piano is a genuine *lieu de mémoire* depicting both the history of slavery in America and the specific story of the Charles family in the South (42–46). As an anniversary present for his wife Ophelia, slaveowner Sutter bought Joel Nolander's piano for one and a half niggers—Berniece's grandmother of the same name and her nine-year-old son, Boy Charles. When Ophelia said she wanted her niggers back, Nolander refused. He offered to buy Willie Boy from Sutter to keep the Charles family together. Sutter refused because he owned everything Doaker's granddaddy, "a worker of wood," carved and made a tidy profit from his slave's labor. Instead Sutter told Willie Boy to carve portraits of Berniece and Boy Charles on the piano. However, Willie Boy, an artist assuming a leadership position as a creator of history like August Wilson himself, decided to tell the whole story and created pictures of the entire family in slavery on the piano.

> DOAKER: Sutter called him up to the house and told him to carve my grandmother and my daddy's picture on the piano for Miss Ophelia. And he took and carved this.... *(DOAKER crosses over to the piano.)* See that right there? That's my grandmother, Berniece. She looked just like that. And he put a picture of my daddy when he wasn't nothing but a little boy the way he remembered him. He made them up out of his memory. Only thing...he didn't stop there. He carved all this. He got a picture of his mama...Mama Esther...and his daddy, Boy Charles.
>
> WINING BOY: That was the first Boy Charles.
>
> DOAKER: Then he put on the side here all kinds of things. See that? That's when him and Mama Berniece got married. They called it jumping the broom. That's how you got married in them days. Then he got here when my daddy was

born…and here he got Mama Esther's funeral…and down here he got Mr. Nolander
taking Mama Berniece and my daddy away down to his place in Georgia. He got all
kinds of things what happened with our family. (44)

Doaker didn't want Berniece to bring the piano to Pittsburgh because he still
"blames himself for not staying behind with Papa Boy Charles" (69), but she
refused to leave it down there in the South. Now Berniece defies Boy Willie's intention to sell the piano, despite the fact that she "ain't touched that
piano the whole time it's been up here." Berniece says:

Mama Ola polished this piano with her tears for seventeen years. For seventeen
years she rubbed on it till her hands bled. Then she rubbed the blood in…mixed it up
with the rest of the blood on it…. (52)

….

When my mama died I shut the top on that piano and I ain't never opened it
since. I was only playing it for her. When my daddy died seem like all her life went
into that piano. She used to have me playing on it…had Miss Eula come in and
teach me…say when I played it she could hear my daddy talking to her. I used to
think them pictures came alive and walked through the house. Sometime late at
night I could hear my mama talking to them. I said that wasn't gonna happen to me.
I don't play that piano cause I don't want to wake them spirits. They never be
walking around in this house.

I got Maretha playing on it. She don't know nothing about it. Let her go on and
be a schoolteacher or something. She don't have to carry all of that with her. She got
a chance I didn't have. I ain't gonna burden her with that piano. (70)

Berniece refuses to part with her heritage, but she's decided not to communicate the family history to Maretha because it would be a heavy burden on her
future as she has to assimilate to white society. At the same time Berniece
refuses to play because she wants to ignore the pain represented and leave the
ancestral spirits undisturbed.

The piano is also, as Michael Morales in "Ghosts on the Piano" points
out, an altar site of blood ritual, for communicating with the ancestors, i.e.,
the totems.[23] Significantly, Doaker sees the "ghost" of its white owner Sutter
three weeks prior to Boy Willie's arrival, the actual time of Sutter's death
falling down a well (after being pushed by Boy Willie?). The ghost tinkles
the piano keys and appears whenever the piano is moved. As long as the instrument remains unused, Sutter's ghost replaces and controls those spirits
depicted on the object itself. In this way, Wilson communicates his belief
that one must know one's past to build a better future; to be truly free, the
ghost of the white man must be exorcised.

---

[23]   Michael Morales, "Ghosts in the Piano," in Alan Nadel, *May All Your Fences Have
Gates: Essays on the Drama of August Wilson* (Iowa City: U of Iowa P, 1994).

For those once considered property and propertyless themselves, the piano physically and metaphorically represents a coming into their own. Stolen from the white man on the fourth of July, the piano is a kind of declaration of independence from white oppression, not unlike Sterling's robbery of Hambone's long-owed ham from Lutz. There is also an historical reflection on African American history in the very pieces of music played on the piano from Boy Willie's Southern boogie woogie to Wining Boy's rambling blues to Doaker's prison and railroad songs to Berniece's refusal to play a Christian hymn to the high culmination of her calling up the ancestors to help Boy Willie conquer and exorcise Sutter's ghost. It is significant that Maretha can only read the sheets, not play by ear like the rest of her family. This is an accommodation to the white culture's process of education at the Settlement House, just as Avery's insistence that Berniece play a Christian hymn on the piano to exorcise Sutter is a useless weapon against white religious hegemony. Once again, finding one's song, Berniece's calling up the ancestral spirits heard like "A rustle of wind blowing across two continents" serves to bring African American history full circle and activate Berniece's use of her legacy.

The Piano Lesson questions how free black men use their legacy. Pride in ownership is part of the lesson here. To own up to and own one's past heritage signifies human worth and identity. Boy Willie's got it right:

> You ought to be talking to Berniece...sitting up there telling Maretha she wished she was a boy. What kind of thing is that to tell a child? If you want to tell her something tell her about that piano. You ain't even told her about that piano. Like that's something to be ashamed of. Like she supposed to go off and hide somewhere about that piano. You ought to mark down on the calendar the day that Papa Boy Charles brought that piano into the house. You ought to mark that day down and draw a circle around it...and every year when it come up throw a party. Have a celebration. If you did that she wouldn't have no problem in life. She could walk around here with her head held high. (90)

Maretha needs to know about and celebrate her family heritage. Papa Boy Charles' declaration of independence from the white man's treatment of his family as property by taking his family history, as depicted on the piano, "home" is a public declaration of the value of his lineage in the face of death itself.

When *The Piano Lesson* opens with Boy Willie knocking at the door and entering shouting at 5:00 a.m., he brings past into the present, the South into the North. Wilson creates the time and the atmosphere:

The dawn is beginning to announce itself, but there is something in the air that belongs to the night. A stillness that is a portent, a gathering, a coming together of something akin to a storm. (1)

Boy Willie's invasion is literally, physically and figuratively a wakeup call to his somnolent kin inside the house and inside the piano and to the lurking "hungry ghost" of Sutter upstairs. There is going to be a disturbance of those very ancestral spirits that terrify Berniece. In addition, there will be an inevitable storm caused by Boy Willie's confrontation of the spirit of the white man who had invaded the Charles family lives with the advent of slavery hundreds of years before.

Wilson preempts any audience reaction towards Sutter's ghost as mere superstition by employing character commentary similar to Seth's "mumbo jumbo" comment about Bynum. Boy Willie first scoffs at the notion of Sutter's ghost as "all in Berniece's head" (13). Wilson, however, has the ghost appear every time there's an attempt to remove the piano from the Charles house and provides a series of witnesses and sound effects for corroboration. The ghost's eerie presence reinforces the building tension between brother and sister over the importance of legacy. Sutter's ghost first appears to Berniece when Boy Willie tells Doaker he's going to sell the piano (12). Sutter frightens her enough to oppose Boy Willie. The ghost appears the second time when Boy Willie and Lymon try to move the piano out of the house. Berniece attacks her brother for "killing and thieving" like Papa Boy Charles, Wining Boy, Doaker, and Crawley and accuses him of killing Crawley (52). The ghost's frightening of Maretha interrupts the sibling battle. Finally in Act Two, Scene 5, Lymon and Boy Willie attempt to take the piano. Sutter's ghost makes his presence known. Despite interruptions by Wining Boy's playing and singing about his lost wife Cleotha and Grace's entrance, brother and sister continue their opposition which ultimately culminates in Berniece pulling Crawley's gun on her own brother (98). Again this is reminiscent of Levee's pulling a gun on Toledo, only here it is one family member against another. Desperation and denial of legacy leads to the misplaced violence of one black person against another "brother."

Wilson dismantles any notion of the effectiveness of Christian exorcism when Avery arrives to bless the piano and the house in Christian fashion calling on Jesus and fails. Boy Willie must defy Sutter directly: "Get your ass out of this house!" and climb up the stairs a ritual three times to confront the ghost. Berniece, seeing Avery's failure, realizes she must help her brother in the "old" African manner of summoning of the ancestors, the spirits in the piano, to come to their aid.

I want you to help me
Mama Berniece
I want you to help me
Mama Esther
I want you to help me
Papa Boy Charles
I want you to help me
Mama Ola
I want you to help me.... (107)

As the sound of the train—that *lieu de mémoire*—approaches, the ghosts of the Yellow Dog take Sutter away. Wilson's message is clear. As he turns black divisiveness into a unified force to confront the white man's centuries-old invasion, a better future for the black man becomes a possibility in America.

In *The Piano Lesson*, August Wilson's use of invasion and cocooning takes on added dimensions. As in *Ma Rainey's Black Bottom*, the bottom floor of the house becomes the arena for confrontation within the black community as brother confronts sister, past enters the present, the South comes to the North. Sutter's ghost, like Sturdyvant in the control booth, terrorizes the inhabitants from above. Boy Willie has to go up three times to confront the ghost on his own level.

Questions of preservation of one's heritage versus assimilation to white society earlier in Ma Rainey's song and Levee's dance music find their counterpart in the conflict between Boy Willie and Berniece. The levels of meaning are, however, much more complex. The debate, housed in music in both plays, finds greater expression through the use of the metaphorical set piece of the piano. More than a three-dimensional family album, the piano is the residence of those Charles ancestral spirits going all the way back to Africa. The contest between Sutter's ghost and the Charles family is a battle over who owns the black man's soul. The family spirits fight with the white man's ghost. The contest is not simply metaphorical, but also real. Sutter exists both in the black man's mind and inhabits the black man's house. Importantly, the battle is an interior one in the house, rather than out in the yard. Berniece supports her brother's ascent up the stairs with all the ancestral force at her disposal. Her newfound discovery of this enabling power frees her from the "bottom of life" (92). Wilson goes much further in his exploration of the black man's journey from property to person, from object to identity

By enclosing the actual conflicts among the black characters who bring their anecdotal history of shared experience onstage within the confines of the house, Wilson has created a cocoon of sorts. Sutter's spiritual invasion into the house itself serves to expose a deeper, psychological problem within the black community. The devaluation and continued terrorization of the black man through slavery and its aftermath has caused a kind of spiritual numbness or acceptance of the *status quo*. Those who have resisted end up in jail like the Parchman Farm. For this reason, the play's conclusion with Berniece and Boy Willie spiritually and physically exorcising the evil remains of slavery, personified in Sutter's ghost, together is cause for celebration. It is the African American community's new fourth of July.

Seven Guitars

> Despite my interest in history, I have always been more concerned with culture, and while my plays have an overall historical feel, their settings are fictions, and they are peopled with invented characters whose personal histories fit within the historical context in which they live.
>
> I have tried to extract some measure of truth from their lives as they struggle to remain whole in the face of so many things that threaten to pull them asunder. I am not a historian. I happen to think that the content of my mother's life—her myths, her superstitions, her prayers, the contents of her pantry, the smell of her kitchen, the song that escaped from her sometimes parched lips, her thoughtful repose and pregnant laughter—are all worthy of art. Hence, *Seven Guitars*.
>
> — August Wilson, Preface to the Play: "A Note from the Playwright," 1995

In *Seven Guitars*, Wilson returns once again to the Pittsburgh neighborhood where he grew up and to blues music, the conduit of black culture in America that helped him find himself as a man and inspire him as an artist to write his first major play, *Ma Rainey's Black Bottom*. Referring to himself as the guitarist,[24] albeit with a typewriter, Wilson is the composer whose seven characters (guitars) give voice to their unique personalities and shared experience as African Americans in the Forties. The time is 1948—a "period of hopefulness" for African Americans who had proven their loyalty during World War II and looked forward to expanded employment as its legacy. Blacks are enormously successful in athletics—note the Joe Louis-Billy Conn heavyweight title match broadcast over the radio—and in music.

Citing the 1940s as the "heyday of urban blues in Chicago," Wilson throws his focus on blues musicians and on one in particular—Floyd "Schoolboy" Barton. Floyd describes Chicago this way:

> Seem like everybody in the world in Chicago. That's the only place for a black man to be. That's where I seen Muddy Waters. I was walking past this club and I heard this music. People was pushing and crowding in the club; seem like the place was

---

24   Hedy Weiss, "Wilson's 'Guitars' Reverberates to the Sound of Black Life," *Chicago Sun-Times,* SHOW Section (January 22, 1995), 1.

busting at the seams. I asked somebody, I say, "Who's that?" They told me, that's Muddy Waters." I took off my hat. I didn't know you could make music sound like that. That told me to say, "The sky's the limit." I told myself say, "I'm gonna play like that one day." I stayed there until they put me out. Mr. T.L. Hall asked me what I wanted to do. I told him I wanted to play at the Hurricane Club. He say he'd fix it.[25]

Vera's warning about putting too much faith in the white manager Mr. T.L. Hall in Act I, Scene 2 goes ignored. Unfortunately it's Hall's involvement in the insurance scam to defraud black folks that causes Floyd's inability to re-possess the band's instruments and drives Floyd to rob Metro Financial Bank to get the money to go to Chicago anyway. Hedy Weiss writes in the *Chicago Sun Times* that Wilson's men and women...have continually been sepa-rated from their 'instruments' of survival. For if it's not their guitar, or their typewriter, it's their land, their money, their job, their family, their music, their history or their sense of self that is in jeopardy."[26]

Jeopardy aptly describes the constant state of the black man and the art-ist. So much is this the case that this play, like *Two Trains Running* preced-ing it in composition, begins with reference to a funeral. Death stalks the black man even in a time of prosperity. As five friends gather after a trip to the cemetery, we discover the man buried was Floyd Barton, hustler and bluesman. Why? How? We ask. Wilson then takes us on a Borgesian trip, a veritable whodunnit, to discover the motivations for such a crime.

> AW: I'm writing a play called *Seven Guitars* which is set in the '40s. It's a murder mystery of sorts about a guy named Floyd Barton.... It's a murder mystery in the sense that by trying to find out who it is that killed Floyd Barton, we have to look at Floyd Barton's life, the social content of his life in Pittsburgh in 1948. The idea came, again from a short story I wrote about a guy who was killed. By going through all the boxes of papers in his room, you discover who he was simply by looking at the contents of his life. So that's what I'm doing, and the play is a flash-back within a flashback within a flashback. It's like a Chinese box where you sud-denly discover it's a flashback, and when you discover where you are, that turns out to be a flashback too. So eventually we arrive at a different place. Beyond that, all the male characters in the play are blues musicians. It's about their relationship to society, to white society and to black society. Whereas in Black society they are car-riers of the culture, a very important part of everyday life, in white society they are vagrants, drunkards, they are constantly harassed by the police, and they've no visi-ble means of support, they're in and out of jail, etc. so there are two different values at work here. The play is about blues musicians, one of whom is Floyd Barton, who has been murdered. But it's really unimportant as to who killed him. It's more im-

25 August Wilson, *Seven Guitars,* 11.
26 Weiss, 1.

portant to find out what's beyond that, about male/female relationships. We see
Floyd Barton and his relationships with various women in these flashbacks.[27]

Once again Wilson explores dramatic form. While he experimented with a
series of monologues and very little action in the preceding play, here he
frames scenes containing past action with beginning and ending scenes in the
present tense of the play and segues from present to past and back with Floyd
Barton's tune "That's All Right" blaring from the radio. Like Lillian Hellman's *The Searching Wind*, this is the only Wilson play utilizing flashbacks
to date. Here, however, there is no physical invasion by the white man. All
the action is contained in the backyard of a rooming house that is populated
by Floyd Barton and six black friends. It is a cocoon. Just as Wilson used
windows as framing devices in the past to focus the attention of those
onstage and in the audience on the action or situation he deemed the most
important aspect of the play, here he also employs time itself to pull the past
into the present onstage, to turn memory into action. The set's one window
here is the portal in the back wall of the house through which the radio blasts
both Floyd Barton's hit single emphasizing the importance of black music,
but also relays the Joe Louis-Billy Conn boxing match in which the Brown
Bomber becomes the heavyweight champion of the world and a role model
for the black man as "king." Wilson frames the play's major conflict expressed through the opposing values of Barton and King Hedley and culmi-
nating in King's murder of Floyd, in something as seemingly simple as two
radio broadcasts. He creates history and invites us to participate in its thriller-
like reconstruction.

Wilson continues his layering of *lieux de mémoire* in *Seven Guitars*. As
usual he constructs history through music, travel routes, jobs, food, and the
setting. All information comes through the life stories of his characters. All
provide living history in that their origins signify the Great Migration. Unlike
Floyd—a Pittsburgh native and singer/electric guitar player, and his lady love
Vera, who's just left her Mama's house in Pittsburgh, the remaining characters all hail from the South. Louise, who runs the rooming house and operates
a beauty parlor, hails from Birmingham, Alabama like her pregnant niece
Ruby. Hedley comes from New Orleans and testifies to his African forebears
and trumpet-playing father who was involved with rum-running and slave
traffic. Canewell also comes from Louisiana where his family cut sugarcane.
He now lives in the Little Haiti section of Pittsburgh, itself a reflection of
both the slave trade route and a black population in the Caribbean. He's the
one who wants a simple life akin to that in the South, provides the others

---

27   Richard Pettengill, "The Historical Perspective," 219, 220.

with recipes and Vera with the golden seal plant, a holistic medicine cure for bleeding similar to those provided by Bynum. Drummer Red Carter comes from Alabama. His womanizing alludes to the continuing break up of the African American family in a search for the new land. Even neighbors like Mrs. Tillery whose rooster wakes up the neighborhood and son robs the bank has a sister in Wheeling, West Virginia. Sarah Devine harkens back to Aunt Ester and rootworker Bynum.

Because his declared subject is bluesmen, musical selections become not only carriers of history, but also a literary means of building the conflict between Floyd and King Hedley. Floyd will do anything, including robbing a bank with his black brother Poochie who's killed by the police, to get the money to further his musical career in Chicago. King Hedley, on the other hand, sees Floyd devaluing his art, his person, and his ancestry, as encapsulated in the accomplishment of Buddy Bolden's trumpet playing, his legacy as part of an African American lineage going back to ancient times in Ethiopia, and his unwillingness to share his money with other members of the black community. There's a major difference between the white man's "give me the money" versus Buddy Bolden's "here go the money." The first alternative reduces all to personal gain in a capitalistic world view whereas the second empowers the black man within his community. It is important to note, however, that the need to express oneself as a person and as an artist is essential to August Wilson. To be the best, to be king, whether as a musician or a boxer, only testifies to the value of the individual and to the worth of the black man. In Wilson's world, the denial of human value in general and major talent in particular causes the outbreak of violence—black against white, black against black.

Since music is the conduit of African American culture for Wilson, it is essential that we look at the story told through music in *Seven Guitars*. Nowhere in his previous plays has he utilized music so elaborately to tell the story of African Americans. Certainly Wilson juxtaposed Ma Rainey's independent voice as the "Mother of Blues" in the Twenties against Levee's attempt to accommodate the new urban black population's interest in dance music to the white man's use of that same music to make money. He also introduced the notion that a black man would turn against his brother, if spurned in the attempt to make music (i.e., sing his own song), to gain the white man's acceptance. As mentioned earlier, Levee's murder of Toledo is a misplaced act of violence against his own community when faced with white rejection. Here in *Seven Guitars*, King Hedley murders Floyd Barton for completely different reasons. To Hedley, Floyd could be King, but won't accept the responsibility. Even if out of desperation, Floyd would rather "do"

Pearl Brown, take advantage of a good woman like Vera and betray Poochie and Canewell, because he doesn't value the roots from which he has sprung. Money as the means of living the high life and having some independence is all-important to Floyd, who refuses to live in that "cold house" of poverty experienced by his beloved mother. On the other hand, his art, however self-ish, seems to be real. In this context, Wilson pits the exceptional talent, the "big man," versus the larger black community and that community against the white hegemony.

Tracking the specific music and its route through the play is a revelatory experience. In Act One, Louise, the play's resident Earth Mother, kicks off the musical sequence with a life-affirming bawdy song—"Anybody here wanna try my cabbage"—to open up the scene where a group of friends gather after returning home from Floyd's funeral. Canewell provides the other side of the picture—that of Death in his "He'll come to your house" song (1). Wilson here establishes musically what he is simultaneously creat-ing with the yard, the arena in which man deals with cosmic forces—the bat-tleground of Life and Death. Once he has introduced this notion, Wilson segues to the now dead Floyd's hit song "That's All Right" coming out of the radio to get to the second scene which begins with Floyd and Vera, both young Pittsburgh natives, dancing to his song.

Scene Two begins the story of Floyd when he was alive. Significantly, the rooster, symbol of the black man's manhood and rural roots, crows while he tries to win Vera back through his sexy dancing style and the lyrics of his love song. Floyd's a World War II vet who describes love at first sight for Vera on Logan Street when he first got home with $47 and a .38 in his pocket. Unfortunately, he later runs off with Pearl Brown to make his first record in Chicago and leaves Vera behind. Floyd may be a good artist, but he's also a "rambling man" in the travelling bluesman tradition. While Canewell got off with handing over the five dollars in his pocket to the po-lice, Floyd has spent the previous ninety days in the workhouse for vagrancy after threatening to burn down the jail. Significantly, he was charged with "worthlessness." It's the same kind of harassment we witness with Jeremy and Lymon. The only apparent solution lies in the letter from Savoy Records with its invitation to "Mister" Floyd Barton to do another recording. Much as actors today move to New York, Floyd wants to go to Chicago. It's "the only place for a black man to be" and particularly for a black musician, such as Muddy Waters or Floyd. Floyd has to figure out how to get his guitar out of pawn to do the job. Louise, administrator of Bella's rooming house and beauty parlor operator, returns with the groceries and registers her disapproval of Floyd. He may be talented and charming, but the audience understands that he doesn't have much moral character.

Scene Three begins with Hedley's emergence from the basement of the house into the yard where he sets up his table and chickens for slaughter. A native of Louisiana, he's set up his own business selling chicken sandwiches, cigarettes, etc. to working men at the mills and at community gatherings such as that for George Butler's death. Hedley actually works at the business Sterling thought of in *Two Trains Running*. He, too is one of Wilson's "warrior spirits." As the rooster crows throughout this scene, Wilson reminds us that Hedley is the King of this barnyard.

Wilson sets up the second main character, his antagonist to Floyd, with the second musical theme. Hedley signals his entrance with a song of his own: "I thought I heard Buddy Bolden say here go the money, King. Take it away" (16). The audience at this point does not understand what this song represents until much later in the play—namely, Act II, scenes i and ii. Hedley's father, who lived in New Orleans when it was a port for slave delivery from Africa and rum-running, named his son King after the great blues horn player Buddy Bolden and thereby gave him divine and African ancestry:

> HEDLEY: My father play the trumpet and for him Buddy Bolden was a god. He was in New Orleans with the boats when he make them run back and forth. The trumpet was his first love. He never forgot that night he heard Buddy Bolden play. Sometime he talked about it. He drink his rum, play his trumpet, and if you were lucky that night he would talk about Buddy Bolden. I say lucky cause you never seen him like that with his face light up and something be driving him from inside and it was a thing he love more than my mother.
>
> That is how he named me king. After King Buddy Bolden. It is not a good thing he named me that. *(Pause.)*
>
> I killed a man once. A black man. I am not worry I killed him.
>
> RUBY: What you kill him for?
>
> HEDLEY: He would not call me King. He laughed to think a black man could be King. I did not want to lose my name, so I told him to call me the name my father gave me, and he laugh.... (67)

The Buddy Bolden song links Hedley to his family ancestry, the Middle Passage, and the quest for identity and self-worth. Continuing the African American legacy is paramount for him. He traces his religion and lineage back to Ethiopia (19) and believes Jesus to be a black man and Mary a Moabite.

> Everybody say Hedley crazy cause he black. Because he know the place of the black man is not at the foot of the white man's boot. Maybe it is not all right in my head sometimes. Because I don't like the world. I don't like what I see from the people. The people is too small. I always want to be a big man. Like Jesus Christ was a big

man. He was the Son of the Father. I too. I am the son of my father. Maybe Hedley
never going to be big like that. But for himself inside…that place where you live
your own special life…I would be happy to be big there. (67–68)

Hedley recognizes how good the music makes him feel about himself. For
this reason, he at first identifies with Floyd's music-making and sees the potential for a "big man" in the next generation. Unlike Floyd, he does not look
to the white man for self-definition.

When Hedley comes out of the basement the second time in the scene,
Floyd greets him by singing "I thought I heard Buddy Bolden say…" (23)
and Hedley responds:

> HEDLEY: What he say?
> FLOYD: He said, "Wake up and give me the money."
> HEDLEY: Naw. Naw. He say, "Come here. Here go the money."
> FLOYD: Well…what he give you?
> HEDLEY: He give me ashes.
> FLOYD: Tell him to give you the money. (23–24)

Hedley believes his dream that Buddy Bolden will give him his father's
money to buy himself a plantation in Pittsburgh so "the white man not going
to tell me what to do no more" (24). He expects a black "big man" to share
the wealth with the rest of the community. Floyd, in contrast, is concerned
only with his own personal advancement. In the dream, the money Buddy
Bolden gives Hedley turns to ashes, prophesying the play's conclusion.

The next piece of music occurs in Act I, Scene 4. Floyd asks Canewell if
he remembers a little rhyme about "in days of old when knights was bold,"
and Canewell then kicks off a sequence of scatological and bawdy verses.
It's a kind of rhythmical juba, itself a *lieu de mémoire*, ranging from primitive times (knights of old) to verbal riddles to strip shows in tents to the policeman killing two boys who'd already killed each other to sweet
watermelons. Watermelons lead to a discussion about handling women and
then Hedley enters. Once again Floyd leads off with "I thought I heard
Buddy Bolden say—" but this time the variations are telling:

> HEDLEY: What he say?
> FLOYD: He said, "Wake up and give me the money."
> HEDLEY: Naw. He say, "Come here. Here go the money."
> FLOYD: What he give you?
> HEDLEY: He didn't give me nothing.
> CANEWELL: You tell him to give you the money. If he don't give it to you,
> come and see me I'll cut him for you.
> HEDLEY: I'll cut him myself.

This dialogue predicts the final scene in which Hedley murders Floyd with the black bossman's primitive weapon, the machete. Immediately following this section, Red Carter gives Hedley a cigar to celebrate the birth of his baby boy to Willa Mae. Hedley then admits to his own hope for offspring and the continuation of the African line: "I hope he grow up and be big and strong like Joe Louis. Maybe one day I too have a son" (40). Again naming is important.

Hedley's response to Canewell's comment that "White folks gonna have a fit with a nigger named Mister. Mr. Mister Carter" evokes Hedley's testimony to African American history.

> HEDLEY: Yes, the bible say Ethiopia shall rise up and be made a great kingdom. Marcus Garvey say the black man is a king. Most people don't know that. Hedley know.... He know himself what blood he got. They say, "Hedley, go on you too serious with that." But Hedley know the white man walk the earth on the black man's back. (40)

Hedley traces the black man's lineage back to ancient Abyssinia (Ethiopia and Arabia), once ruled by the black Queen of Sheba who bore a son of Solomon. Eventually Christianized, Ethiopia became the first African nation to repel European colonization in its defeat of the Italians at Adowa in 1896.

> The legacy of Ethiopia has had a great effect on the Black world.... The news of this African state under an African king defeating a European army spread like wildfire. Everywhere throughout the Black Diaspora, in Africa, the West Indies, South America, Europe, and North America, Ethiopia became a symbol of power, freedom, and redemption. In November 1930 Rastafari Makonnen was crowned Haile Selassie I, Power of the Holy Trinity, 225th Emperor of the Solomonic Dynasty, Elect of God, King of Kings, Lord of Lords, Conquering Lion of the Tribe of Judah. Emperor Haile Selassie declared his monarchy the oldest continuous monarchy in the world tracing his descent back to the union of Solomon and Sheba.[28]

Hedley also cites Marcus Garvey, the famous Jamaican labor-organizer and founder of the Universal Negro Improvement and Conservation Association and African Communities League (UNIA) who supported black businesses and black emigration to Africa. He went to prison for "mail fraud." L'Ouverture, the "Liberator of Haiti," was actually the descendant of an African King who had been sold into slavery. He led the French against the British in Haiti, but Napoleon, fearful of his power, incarcerated him. He died there in 1803. Both leaders were imprisoned by the white man. Floyd's response denies the value of Hedley's list of role models for the black com-

---

[28]   KAM Ancient Abyssinia, p. 6) located at <http://www.geocities.com/College Park/Classroom/9912/ancientabyssinia.html>)

munity and puts him in direct conflict with the King. "The only thing I want you to do is get out my way." Hedley warns him: "You watch what Hedley say" (41).

In Scene Four, after a discussion in which Floyd finally agrees to get Red's drums out of pawn, the four men have a jam session. Hedley once again goes off to the basement and brings out the elements necessary to make his "one string," a primitive instrument harkening back to Africa. Hedley says that he learned to play from his Grandfather who said he could hear his mother pray through the sound. This comment inspires Floyd, whose devotion to his own mother is paramount, to sing the "Our Father" after referring to another favorite "Old Ship of Zion," the same hymn Avery wants Berniece to play on the piano. Floyd's comment that his mother's buried in Greenwood leads to Canewell's African-style listing of all the people out there they know: George Butler, Jack Harding, Ed Weatherby, Uncle Doc, Aunt Lil, Raymond Polk—all in the poor section. This past genealogy builds up to the radio's announcement of the latest king—"Joe Louis, the Heavy-weight Champion of the World, defends his title..." (51). For one brief scene, the group comes together in a musical celebration of family and black achievement in sports.

Joe Louis's victory over Billy Conn elicits a huge response from the group in Scene Five. In ritualistic fashion, they begin circling the yard and chanting "the Brown Bomber." Soon this becomes the Joe Louis Victory Walk and the Joe Louis Shuffle. However, when Red Carter encourages Vera in the suggestive, hip-grinding "Jump jump here" (53), Floyd pulls a gun on Red. Only Ruby's arrival stops the impending violence, a precursor to Floyd's turning on Canewell in Scene 8.

Act II, Scene 1 opens with both musical themes going simultaneously. It is a kind of musical competition between Floyd's "That's All Right" from the radio and Hedley singing "Buddy Bolden" while wrapping up the grilled chicken sandwiches he's made along with eggs (the classic fertility symbol), cigarettes, and candy bars. Desirous of an heir, Hedley opens up to Ruby, tells her about his name (70) and his dreams of being a "big man" like Buddy Bolden. Ruby could help him.

> And maybe my child, if it be a boy, he would be big like Moses. I think about that. Somebody have to be the father of the man to lead the black man out of bondage. Marcus Garvey have a father. Maybe if I could not be like Marcus Garvey then I could be the father of someone who would not bow down to the white man. Maybe I could be the father of the messiah. I am fifty-nine years old and my time is running out. Hedley is looking for a woman to lie down with and make his first baby. Maybe...maybe you be that woman for me. Maybe we both be blessed. (68)

Ruby rejects Hedley and he goes off to the basement to get boxes of candy. When he's gone, Floyd arrives and hustles her. Hedley doesn't like the situation and questions Floyd about going to the pawnshop to get his guitar. When Floyd admits he doesn't have the money to retrieve it, Hedley sings "Buddy Bolden" because he thinks the white man has a plan to destroy Floyd and sees the bluesman's desperation. He'll take money wherever he can find it—from Buddy Bolden, High John the Conqueror, Yellow Jack, Brer Rabbit, Uncle Ben—even figures that exist only in folklore. Witnessing Floyd's low self-esteem coupled with his running after Ruby, Hedley tries to get Floyd to behave like a king:

> You are like a king! They look at you and they say, "This one...this one is the pick of the litter. This one we have to watch. We gonna put a mark on this one. This one we have to crush down like the elephant crush the lion!" You watch your back! The white man has a big plan against you. Don't help him with his plan. He look to knock you down. He say, "That one!" Then they all go after you. You best be careful! (71)

Wilson uses the classic example of signifyin(g) wherein the monkey badmouths the elephant to the lion. The lion then confronts the elephant, but the elephant trounces him to explain the white man's intention to destroy leadership in the black community. For Hedley, money, the bartering agent that signifies success for the white man and American society, doesn't define the "big man." A man's ability to give it away, like Aunt Ester, to help others indicates his real worth as a human being.

Scene Four presents Hedley singing a different tune. Irate over the city's report that he's got tuberculosis and should go to the sanitarium, Hedley's gone to his black bossman Roberts for help. He returns with a machete "ready for the white man when he come to take him away." He declares his independence and also expresses his sexual urgency in "For the pussin (person/pussy) belong to me" (85–86). He dances around the yard. He tells the story of accusing his father of doing nothing in his life of importance like Toussaint L'Ouverture and his father's response of kicking him in the mouth. Marcus Garvey helped him get his voice back and forgive his father who, already dead and unable to hear his son's confession, appears to him in a dream promising Buddy Bolden's arrival with some money to buy a plantation. Machete in hand, the scene closes with Hedley ready to take on the white man.

Scene Five opens with Hedley rocking back and forth while chanting "Ain't no grave...can hold my body down," indicating his continuing defiance when faced with Death and the possibility of resurrection. His spirit will not die, but will join the ancestral ranks. Hedley testifies to his lineage, thereby becoming a verbal *lieu de mémoire*. He begins to walk around the yard in a circle shouting: "The black man is not a dog! He is the Lion of Judah! He is the mud God make his image from. Ethiopia shall stretch forth her wings!" (88). Hedley offers himself to Ruby declaring:

> I am a warrior. When I am in this dust, my knees buckle from war, not from a woman! I offer you a kingdom...the flesh of my flesh, my seven generations...and you laugh at me! You laugh at Joe Louis' father! I offer you to be the Lily of the Valley. To be Queen of Sheba. Queen of the blackman's kingdom. You think I am a clown. I am the Lion of Judah! (88)

Ruby rescues Hedley from his frenzied response to the denial of his value by both blacks and whites by giving herself to him and convincing him the baby is his. Hence, Hedley believes his line will continue so he can freely go to Church and the sanitarium later.

Scene Six discloses Floyd burying the stolen money in the garden. We learn he's bought a new guitar, just like the one owned by Muddy Waters, a dress and tickets to Chicago for Vera, and contacted the President of Savoy Records. Scene 8 deals with news of the great success at the Mother's Day dance at the Blue Goose as they all return from the club. Louise sings "That's All Right" like the tune from a hit show. In a manner similar to Masha and Vershinin in Chekhov's *The Three Sisters*, Floyd and Vera joke with musical titles about the evening they're going to spend together in bed. Floyd's "Good Rockin' Tonight" elicits her "Sixty Minute Man" (102–103).

As the music dies away in Scene 8, the play's conflict reaches its climax. Declaring that the stolen money is his and no one else's, Floyd pulls a gun on Canewell. When Canewell realizes Poochie died in the robbery attempt of Metro Financial, he gives Floyd back the money and leaves. Floyd has betrayed the community. Hedley, believing Floyd to be Buddy Bolden, asks him to give him the money promised in the dream. Floyd selfishly refuses and shoves Hedley to the ground. Hedley exits into the basement, grabs his machete and severs Floyd's windpipe with one blow. Hedley, the King of the Jungle, closes the scene with another version of his song's lyrics: "This time, Buddy...you give me the money" (104). No sharing, no life.

Wilson employs "That's All Right" on the radio to segue from past to present as we return to the friends gathering after Floyd's funeral. After Ruby and Red, Louise and Vera exit, only Canewell and Hedley are left. The silence between them swells. Then we hear the last musical themes repeated ("I thought I heard Buddy Bolden say..."). This time Hedley "holds up a handful of crumpled bills" which "slip through his fingers and fall to the ground like ashes" (107). Again Hedley sings "I thought I heard Buddy Bolden say..." three times. The implication is that he thought he heard, but he heard wrong. Once again, black man turns against black man. The killing is an empty victory. Neither cultural assimilation nor cultural separatism works. His father's money cannot make Hedley a "big man." Money cannot make up for the failure to understand and believe in one's self-worth or the value of community.

The setting of this play is integral to an understanding of *Seven Guitars*. Wilson carefully points out that the action of the play takes place in the backyard of a two-storied brick house, owned by Bella, where Vera, Louise, and Hedley have their own individual apartments reached by shabby stairs. No one here is financially independent enough to own his or her own property—either the house or their instruments. There is one window from which emanates radio broadcasts of Floyd's music and boxing bouts. Popular music and professional sports are accepted modes of achievement for the black man. Importantly, a cellar door leads into a basement where Hedley stores his gear. It hints at the past and the dark underbelly of 1948 urban African American life. Off to the side at the rear of the yard is a contraption made of bricks, wood, and corrugated sheet metal. It is "a primitive mortician table of sorts" where Hedley kills his chickens and turkeys and reminds the viewer of Bynum's pigeon slaughtering in *Joe Turner's Come and Gone*. In the hot muggy summer nights of 1948, a card table is often set up in the yard surrounded by an "eclectic mix of chairs" and lit via gerry-rigged extension cords run from Vera's apartment. Wilson says:

> The yard in this play is the one I remember from the house I grew up in. I wanted it to suggest a bullring, the pit of a slaughterhouse full of blood and guts, even if it was only from chickens. It's a garden, but it's also a killing field, a cemetery, a sacred place where blood is shed.[29]

And the scene of Floyd's murder as well. Floyd's burying the stolen money in the ground and simultaneously exposing the roots of the goldenseal plant, Canewell's gift to Hedley, is truly an ironic touch. A native American herb, goldenseal's yellow root was used to stop bleeding and act as an antiseptic. The uncovering of its roots deadens its healing powers and reveals the source of the damage—the hidden money. Floyd's desperate greed will cause the death of Poochie, a fight with Canewell ending with Floyd's pulling a gun on his friend, and Hedley's murder of Floyd.

There is no place more appropriate for blood sacrifice or the celebration of new life (Willa Mae's son), love (or sex), and accomplishment (Joe Louis) than the ancient earth, the dirt of the backyard. Ultimately, the yard in Wil-

---

[29] Weiss, 1.

son's play takes on the attributes of ritual theater as Wole Soyinka describes
it:

> Ritual theater...establishes the spatial medium not merely as a physical area for
> simulated events but as a manageable contraction of the cosmic envelope within
> which man...fearfully exists. And this attempt to manage his special awareness
> makes every manifestation in ritual theater a paradigm for the cosmic human condi-
> tion.[30]

Despite the fact that Wilson builds a neighborhood cocoon for his black
characters to express their true feelings, the desperate struggle for survival in
white America suggested by T.L. Hall's insurance fraud, Savoy Records'
exploitation of black musicians and random imprisonment of blacks, pene-
trates the environment and contributes to its shattering. While Hedley declares that "The rooster is the king of the barnyard. He like the black man. He
king" (61), he ends up killing it in a kind of ceremonial ritual which punishes
the black man for betraying his noble legacy and forecasts his murder of
Floyd.

> HEDLEY: Soon you mark my words when god ain't making no more niggers.
> They too be a done thing. This here rooster born in the barnyard. He learn to cock
> his doodle-do. He see the sun, he cry out so the sun don't catch you with your hand
> up your ass or your dick stuck in your woman. You hear this rooster you know you
> alive. You be glad to see the sun cause there come a time sure enough when you see
> your last day and this rooster you don't hear no more. *(He takes out a knife and cuts
> the rooster's throat.)* That be for the living. Your black ass be dead like the rooster
> now. You mark what Hedley say. *(He scatters the blood in a circle.)* This rooster too
> good live for your black asses. *(He throws the rooster on the ground.)* Now he good
> and right for you. (64)

Wilson states: "I see that rooster in direct relation to blacks in America....
Once cotton was no longer king, once blacks had to be paid for their labor,
there was suddenly no use for 35 million people in this country."[31] Displaced
from his original agrarian habitat in Africa and his migration on Highway 61
from Mississippi to Chicago, the black man (the rooster) is lost to himself
and his purpose.

World War II raises the black man's expectations regarding his rights to
opportunity in America. However, when his economic slavery continues and
many things "threaten to pull him asunder," he resorts to violence against his
oppressor's institutions and against his own black brother or sister. Even

---

[30] Wole Soyinka, *Myth, Literature, and the African World* (Cambridge: Cambridge UP,
1976), 41 (cited in Rocha, "American History," 127).
[31] Weiss, 1.

though he professes love and respect for his mother whose own lineage goes back to the Queen of Sheba or Esther who saved the Jews from genocide, the black man here has lost his sense of self-worth and the support system of a valuable ancestral lineage. Instead he carries weapons (also one of the play's *lieux de mémoire*) for self-defense. Hedley's got his kitchen knife and eventual machete. Canewell carries a pocket knife. Floyd and Red have guns. Even Louise has a .38 under her pillow, a trace of the man who abandoned her. Floyd buys into the notion that America won the war because of bigger guns and the atomic bomb (44). Floyd Barton's "selling out" of his art (song), betrayal of both Vera and his black brother in the robbery, and his selfish attempt to keep the ill-gotten money for himself to further his career, signifies the debasement of African communal values and individual identity in the mad scramble for the fast life, fame, and fortune in Chicago.

Yet the backyard belongs to King Hedley. Appropriately so. He is a sick man. His rent is late. He still goes to Sarah Degree for root tea. He hungers for sex and offspring. He is a living *lieu de mémoire*, the human repository of all the conflicting elements that have tortured the African American and driven him to the brink of lunacy. Hedley contains within himself all the ruptures that have occurred in African American history/culture and bears witness to the violent insanity such a burden provokes.

Two Trains Running

August Wilson: "I grew up without a father. When I was 20 I went down onto Centre Avenue to learn from the community how to be a man. My education comes from the years I spent there. Mostly I'd listen to the older guys, because I was impressed. Here was a guy who lived 60 years—and I didn't think I was going to make it to the next year.

My plays stem from impressions I formed on The Hill in the '50s and '60s.... Those were times of great struggle and change for blacks.[32]

....

The play does not speak to these so-called red lettered events of the sixties, because at the time all of that was going on—the assassination of Martin Luther King and Bobby Kennedy and all the anti-war administrations, etc.—people were still living their lives. You still had to go to work everyday, you still had to pay your rent, you still had to put food on the table. And those events, while they may have in some way affected the character of society as a whole, didn't reach the average person who was concerned with just simply living. And so in *Two Trains* I was more concerned with those people and what they were doing and how they were dealing with it, than I was with writing a "sixties" play.[33]

---

[32]   "The Hill District: People: August Wilson at <http://alphaclp.clpgh.org/clp/exhibit/ neighborhoods/hill/hill_n102.html>
[33]   August Wilson to Richard Pettengill, 207.

As you get older there are some things that you can see more clearly than you could five years ago and certainly more clearly than you could twenty years ago. I'm the kind of person who likes to look back—I benefit from the historical perspective. I can see myself as a young man, when we were trying to alter the relationship of Black Americans to the society in which we lived. One of the ways of doing that, of course, was to get some power, and also to alter our shared expectations of ourselves. But one of the things I realized as I was writing *Two Trains Running* was that we had isolated ourselves from the Sterlings of the world. We had isolated ourselves from that energy. Somehow by trying to speak for the people we got way out in front of the people and left the people behind; we forgot to follow them where they were going. It was a romanticized vision; it was part of being young, part of youth. We were all 23, 25, all young men engaged in a society. What I would hope is that young men today are still involved in trying to alter their relationship to the society which now, more than ever, needs to be altered.[34]

In *Two Trains Running*, August Wilson writes from a multi-layered temporal perspective—his own experiences in the Hill District as a youth, his participation in the Black Power movement of the Sixties, a general knowledge of the turbulent racial and international (Vietnam) context of the period, and a 1990s mature look at what past events, personal and public, mean to him in his individual role as an African American, in his communal role as a responsible artist/shaman to Blacks, and in his societal role as an American citizen. Wilson's focus is now, as always, on the lives of ordinary Black Americans. It is not on the larger context, the turbulent documented ruptures in American history of Vietnam, Watts and other race riots, the march on Washington, and the multiple assassinations of civil rights leaders, both black and white—the two Kennedys, Martin, and Malcolm X.

Talking about *Two Trains Running*, Lloyd Richards says:

August has done here what he had done in all the plays he has written. His plays have centered themselves in a decade and have illuminated the life of an oppressed people during that time. He has not approached the plays as historical chronologies of the events of a time, or even as dialogues on the problems of a time. He has approached everything through characters, characters who any of us may have encountered or avoided encountering on the street. He has put them in a position where we can get to know them through their attempts to deal with the issues of their time as they affect their everyday lives. And in their struggle to live, to survive, to thrive, to respect themselves, one begins to perceive these people in their time; you see the history flowing to the time and flowing from it as it affects the lives and the decisions of those characters.[35]

---

34   Pettengill, 220–21.
35   *Ibid.*, 103.

Key characters observe the outside world through the door window in Memphis' diner. Sterling bears witness to the crowd of negroes lining up to see the dead evangelist Prophet Samuel at West's funeral parlor across the street[36] and Memphis and Wolf observe Holloway watch Hambone demanding his ham from Lutz, as he's done every day for the past 9 1/2 years. As Wilson declares, "the point of the play is that by 1969 nothing has changed for the black man. You talk about King and Malcolm, but by 1969, as it says in the play, both are dead. The reality is that Sterling's just out of the penitentiary and someone like Holloway, who is sixty-five, has been struggling his whole life and still has nothing to show for it."[37] For Wilson, these two main characters (Sterling and Memphis) bear witness to the fact embodied in the Lutz/Hambone incident that time has stood still for the ordinary black man. Simultaneously Wilson is schooling his audience because Hambone also "shows us that a new black man was created in the 1960s who would not accept a chicken."[38] For today's audience and the black community, it's time to "pick up the ball" dropped during the Sixties; Wilson: "I think it was an absolutely great time, much needed, and I'm sorry to see it dissipated...it was all a part of the people's lives: they had been given a platform."[39] The time has passed for blacks to accept white evangelical religion (Prophet Samuel) and white judgments regarding the economic worth of the black man's labor and property (Lutz).

Wilson advances possible solutions to the characters' bleak circumstances in Sterling's energetic solidarity and support of Hambone's defiance; in Memphis's picking up the ball by bending the rules of the white hegemony to suit his life goals of reconnecting with the South and owning his own business to insure his continuing independence, and in the old African healing of Aunt Ester (Ancestor) who connects men with their souls through story-telling and tossing money to the river gods.

> MEMPHIS: Aunt Ester clued me on this one. I went up there and told her my whole life story. She say, "If you drop the ball, you got to go back and pick it up. Ain't no need in keeping running, cause if you get to the end zone it ain't gonna be a touchdown." She didn't say it in them words but that's what she meant. She told me... "You got to go back and pick up the ball." That's what I'm gonna do. I'm going back to Jackson and see Stovall. If he ain't there, then I'm gonna see his son. He enjoying his daddy's benefits he got to carry his daddy's weight. I'm going on back up to Jackson and pick up the ball. (109)

---

36 August Wilson, *Two Trains Running*, 21.
37 Sylvie Drake, *Los Angeles Times*, 17 January 1992; quoted in Rocha, "American History," 130.
38 Rocha, "American History," 130.
39 Powers, 52.

Memphis has a job of his own making; Sterling, fresh out of prison, doesn't. Sterling may use his gun if he can't find a job whereas Memphis's business has kept him off the street. One may resort to violence to keep alive, but the other will develop a new set of rules entirely to win an equitable price for his property from the City and either return to the South to retrieve his land or establish an even larger restaurant owned and run by black folks on Centre Avenue.

While Wilson continues his exploration of the unique African American past, he is also looking for new ways to incorporate this information within the new American Civil Rights movement. The latter with its stress on constitutional rights for all guaranteeing humane treatment and equal opportunity in pay and employment aligns him with Lillian Hellman's values—both cultural and economic. Like Hambone, he wants the white man to recognize his worth. Torn between Martin Luther King's Gandhian approach of nonviolence and Malcolm X's often violent black power, where is the solution to the day-to-day dilemma of black folks in America, Wilson asks.

To explore the consequences of the loss of black leaders, economic oppression, and the racial turbulence of the decade on ordinary black folk, Wilson uses his usual technique of layering *lieux de mémoire*—music, travel routes and jobs, timely details, food, and most heavily in this play, anecdotal history, and the setting. There are three specific musical references in *Two Trains Running*—the title itself and the "Queen of Soul" Aretha Franklin's version of "Take a Look" emanating from the miraculously working, formerly out-of-order jukebox, and underscoring one of the small bits of action in the play when Sterling kisses Risa, and Sterling's rendition of "Wake Up, Pretty Mama" after his visit to Aunt Ester. The two musical selections span past and present from blues to contemporary pop.

Wilson takes his title from an old railroad blues song composed by McKinley "Muddy Waters" Morganfield about a black man caught in a love affair with "another man's wife." He wants to take a train, but none goes in the right direction.[40] As in *The Piano Lesson*, the train connects North and South, urban Pittsburgh and rural Mississippi, Life and Death. Romare Bearden, whose paintings inspired Wilson and often incorporated train images, stresses their importance this way: "Trains are so much a part of Negro life. Negroes lived near the tracks, worked on the railroads and the trains carried them north during the migration."[41] Shannon discusses the great impact

---

[40] Shannon, 171.

[41] Quoted in Joan Fishman, "Romare Bearden, August Wilson and the Traditions of African Performance," in Alan Nadel, *May All Your Fences Have Gates: Essays on the Drama of August Wilson* (Iowa City: U of Iowa P, 1994), 139.

railroads had upon "the sociology, demographics and the economics of black life," its metaphorical use by the blues singer who used its emotional power over an audience to evoke the breakup of families and male/female relationships (171).

Wilson extends the line "two trains running, neither one going my way. One running by night, one run by day" to express the

> two ideas in the play...have confronted black America since the Emancipation, the ideas of cultural assimilation and cultural separatism. These were, in my mind, the two trains. I wanted to write a play about a character for whom neither of these trains were working. He had to build a new railroad in order to get to where he's going....[42]

In *Two Trains Running*, Wilson concentrates on the elaborate storytelling, the ritual talk of seven characters who regularly patronize Memphis Lee's Home Food Restaurant, a diner in the Hill District of Pittsburgh. "What we witness is not a play about the '60s, but a form of oral history, in which we're invited to eavesdrop on the timeless continuum of the African American experience."[43] Wilson experiments with talk, not action, to invite the audience into the daily lives of urban African Americans. "The glorious storytelling serves not merely as picturesque, sometimes touching and often funny theater but as a penetrating revelation of a world hidden from view to those outside it."[44] He seduces us in the audience to cross the color line by engaging us in the "loudtalking" mode of "signifyin(g)" wherein both those onstage and in the audience become the addressees of the onstage speakers. As Michael Rocha points out in his discussion of Holloway's "stacking niggers" speech, "The historical point of *Two Trains Running* is not merely to offer a salutary addition or correction to an already existing American History. Instead the play offers its audience the opportunity to 'do' American history by including them as participants in a ritual of signifyin(g) through which they become self-conscious about their odd disconnectedness to a black experience around which W.E.B. DuBois put it, 'the history of the land has centered for thrice a hundred years.'"[45] Wilson's portrait gallery of garrulous elders entertain and school us with monologues pulsing with musical rhythm, ideas, and incidents which both create history and involve us in its creation. As Wilson says:

---

[42]   Pettingill, 208.
[43]   David Ansen, "Of Prophets and Profits: August Wilson's '60s," *Newsweek* (27 April 1992), 70 (cited in Shannon, 171).
[44]   Frank Rich, "August Wilson Reaches the 60s With Witnesses From a Distance," *The New York Times* (April 12, 1992), 13, 17.
[45]   Rocha, "American History," 117.

The talk is the whole point because I'm dealing with a culture that has an oral tradition. You want talky, go read Chekhov. These stories mean something different to these people [in *Two Trains*]. They're not just passing the time or entertaining themselves, they're creating and preserving themselves. In the oral tradition, stories are the way history gets passed down, so they better be told right. By "right" I mean in a way that's memorable. Africans judge a storyteller by how long he can hold an audience.[46]

Only three characters speak of their roots in the Old South. Memphis, the self-made man former farmer and now black business owner, came to Pittsburgh in Depression 1936, the same time as Boy Willie in *The Piano Lesson*. Memphis, in his fifties, had already bought his own farm in Jackson, Mississippi and was run off it by whites in 1931. Abandoned by her family, his mother died in the South and he was too poor to attend the funeral. Holloway, 65, who's got cousins in Jackson, went to Aunt Ester, the neighborhood's 322-year-old black sage whose years stand for the history of blacks in America and whose wisdom enables people to heal themselves by telling their stories, because he hated his grandfather who couldn't wait to pick cotton for the white God in heaven. Hambone, in his forties, hails from Alabama, but no one knows his name. "Hambone ain't had no people. Most anybody know about him is he come from Alabama. Don't even know his right name" (90).

All the characters share experience as Northern urban blacks trying to survive in Pittsburgh. Memphis, father of four, has been deserted by his wife. He owns the restaurant and takes in tenants upstairs for additional income and for security against fire. Wolf is the community numbers runner who urges poor blacks to get ahead through gambling. Holloway is a retired housepainter and lives on social security. His relative security allows him to be the diner's resident know-it-all and pundit. West, former bootlegger and numbers runner, has made a fortune as the undertaker for all blacks in the neighborhood and owns half the real estate. Hambone is the retarded man who daily confronts Lutz to give him the ham promised for painting the fence. Risa is the young cook/waitress who works in the restaurant and has scarred her legs to prevent men from only seeing her as a sex object.

The intruder, who's not really new to the community, is thirty-year-old Sterling, a recently-released convict and former bank robber who's looking for a job. The duffers remember him as the Hendricks boy who robbed the bank and got caught spending the money immediately afterwards. To Risa—his friend Rodney's younger sister—Sterling communicates his past history as an orphan at the Toner Institute and his future dreams for marriage,

---

[46]   Rocha, "American History," 126.

a job, a car, and money in his pocket. Sterling had taken Holloway's advice to see Aunt Ester, threw his money in the river, and ended up singing "Wake up, Pretty Mama" (98). While he invites Risa on a date to the Malcolm X rally, his naïveté is obvious. He can, however, teach Hambone Malcolm's important slogan: "United we stand... Divided we fall" (64). While Memphis won't support Sterling's idea of selling chicken sandwiches at the steel mill and opposes Risa's giving food to Hambone, Sterling—Wilson's "warrior spirit"—tries to rectify the perceived inequity towards Hambone when he bleeds for a brother and steals the ham for Hambone's coffin. It's the young generation that understands that black folks need to support each other.

On the other hand, the diner's "regulars" communicate all the neighborhood gossip through stories that reflect family fragmentation and economic oppression. They judge Prophet Samuel's alliance with Mellon, representative of white banking interests, and Negroes who attend his laying-out to rub his head and thereby find money in the way the dead man did. The Lone Wolf delineates the Alberts' control of the numbers racket. Holloway advocates Aunt Ester's importance in making you right with yourself by getting your "soul washed" (24), and Memphis ignores the Malcolm X rally as both faddish and useless because Malcolm's dead like other black leaders. They believe that Sterling, who purchases a gun from Wolf and can't get a job at Hendricks, J&L Steel, or Boykins junkyard, is doomed to return to prison.

Memphis addresses the history of the Great Migration, its resultant family breakup and the loss of Northern urban black communities due to the demise of neighborhood businesses during the Sixties.

> WOLF: When they gonna tear it [the restaurant] down?
> HOLLOWAY: You know how the city is. They been gonna tear this whole block down for the last twenty years.
> MEMPHIS: They told me to be downtown Tuesday. They liable to wait another twenty years before they tear it down, but I'm supposed to be down there Tuesday and find out how much they gonna give me.
> WOLF: What you gonna do when they tear it down?
> MEMPHIS: Ain't nothing to do. Unless I do like West and go into the undertaking business. I can't go out there in Squirrel Hill [the white neighborhood] and open up a restaurant. Ain't nothing gonna be left around here. Supermarket gone. Two drugstores. The five and ten. Doctor done moved out. Dentist done moved out. Shoestore gone. Ain't nothing gonna be left but these niggers killing one another. That don't never go out of style. West gonna get richer and everybody else gonna get poorer. At one time you couldn't get a seat in here. Had the jukebox working and everything. Time somebody get up somebody sit down before they could get out the door. People coming from everywhere. Everybody got to eat and everybody got to sleep. Some people don't have stoves. Some people don't have nobody to cook for them. Men whose wives done died and left them. Cook for them thirty years and lay

down and die. Who's gonna cook for them now? Somebody got to do it. I order four
cases of chicken on Friday and Sunday it's gone. Fry it up. Make a stew. Boil it.
Add some dumplings. You couldn't charge more than a dollar. But then you didn't
have to. It didn't cost you but a quarter. People used to come from all over. The man
used to come twice a week to collect the jukebox. He making more money than I
am. He pay seventy-five cents for the record and he make two hundred dollars off it.
If it's a big hit he's liable to make four hundred. The record will take all the quarters
you can give it. It don't never wear out. The chicken be gone by Sunday. It ain't
nothing like that now. I'm lucky if I go through a case a chicken a week. That's alright. I'll take that. I ain't greedy. But if they wanna tear it down they gonna have to
meet my price. (10)

Memphis, however, is the one who builds a new railroad. He forges a
new path in utilizing a white lawyer to get the price he wants for the diner
and simultaneously plans to "pick up the ball" by reclaiming his land in the
South or possibly opening a new, larger restaurant on Centre Avenue. This
time Wilson focuses on an economic situation in which blacks struggle for
survival and for self-definition. Significantly, the diner is the site of a black-
owned business, like Becker's gypsy cab station in *Jitney*. A cocoon for its
Hill denizens, Memphis's diner is a way station akin to the Holly's boardinghouse, which was primarily a locus for spiritual reconnection and only secondarily a business serving those fleeing the South during the Great
Migration. Memphis had arrived as part of that mass exodus and began sup-
plying newly-arrived black migrants with warmth, shelter and home food,
listed on the diner's blackboard with 1969 prices—details no doubt remem-
bered by Wilson from his own jobs as a short-order cook.

In *Two Trains Running*, Wilson returns once again to his beloved Hill
District in Pittsburgh. His setting is "a small restaurant with four stools, a
counter, and three booths lined against one wall." All action occurs within
the restaurant located across the street from West's funeral Home and Lutz's
Meat Market, black and white businesses. Wilson uses the window framing
device—seen before in Seth and Bertha's viewing of Bynum performing his
rituals outside—to establish the play's focus. In *Two Trains Running,* the
door window looking out at the neighborhood and throwing into relief both a
questionable death-dealing, money-grubbing ethic evident in Prophet Samuel's funeral line and Hambone's demand for just payment for work done in
a black/white environment outside.

As in *Jitney* (set in 1971), Memphis Lee's Home Food Restaurant is
slated for demolition, ostensibly as part of Pittsburgh's downtown rehabilita-
tion. The set thus acts as a three-dimensional metaphor or *lieu de mémoire*
representing the break up and disintegration of the black community left behind in the ghettoes of Northern industrial cities and a site for discussing pos-

sible solutions to the economic slavery resulting in the violence and drug abuse of the unemployed. As Memphis says:

> I had seen a way for me to take off my pistol. I got my deed and went right home...took off my pistol and hung it up in the closet. West got mad when he found out L.D. sold me the building. He been trying to buy it from me ever since. He walked in the next day and offered me eight thousand dollars for it. That was a good price. But see...he didn't know it had come to mean more to me than that. I had found a way to live the rest of my life. (9)

The diner houses a motley group of survivors whose general old age likens them to a group of elders in the African tradition passing on their oral history to all young people who have gathered to listen, including the unskilled, jobless ex-con Sterling and the larger public in the audience. Not jaded by past experience, Sterling and Risa still hold forth the notion that love and compassion are possible. No white character ever enters this location except in conversation. Hence, the diner houses what James Baldwin called "the field of manners and ritual intercourse" that centers upon and sustains Black American life.

Following Baraka's influence, Wilson assumes the responsibility of shaman/teacher in reassembling and shaping a new meaningful identity for his own people and presenting the richness of an African American heritage within the diversity of American society. To do so, he takes his racially mixed American audience into a largely black enclave where his black characters can freely discuss their *status quo*. He exposes the disruptive fragmentation of African American culture. At the same time, Wilson theatrically presents possible solutions to the dilemmas within the black community in the release of songs of identity, the sharing of experience, and new approaches towards jobs and better use of resources.

Freedom and Responsibility: Emergence of a New American Identity

In summary, both Lillian Hellman and August Wilson rewrite history in the fictional format of theatre. Knowing that the audience goes to the theatre because it wants to be there, these two authors do much more than simply entertain. Theatrical performance provides them the opportunity to exercise their craft as playwrights and to rewrite history as they see it. Their plays attempt to make an audience aware of the diverse makeup of our society at the same time that they advocate equal rights and opportunity for all its members regardless of gender or race. Oppression from within or without is intolerable to both.

Both utilize their stage settings as *lieux de mémoire* housing "moments of danger" for the American nation and its citizenry. Their perspectives do, however, vary. Hellman concerns herself with any invasion of the rights to free expression or equal opportunity. She mines her family memories and work as reporter and union activist to re-awaken America to its own history and to an awareness of self-interested irresponsibility on both the home and international fronts. Her characters, like Whalen versus Rodman/Ellicott in *Days to Come* or Kurt versus Teck, seeking or threatening freedom to both the individual American or to the nation as a whole, literally invade the space. Hellman, for the most part, locates her plays in specific American geographical areas including the educational incubator of the New England Dobie-Wright Girls School of *The Children's Hour* versus the social establishment of the Tilford living room; the wealthy midwestern home of factory owner Rodman and contrasting bare-bones strikers' office of *Days to Come*; the aristocratic Southern mansions taken over by the *nouveau riche*, greedy would-be industrialists, the Hubbards in *The Little Foxes* and *Another Part of the Forest*; the homes of the Washington, D.C. political elite of Justice Farrelly and Diplomat Hazen or the World War II hotel/restaurant locations of Paris, Rome and Berlin in *The Searching Wind*; and finally the shabby cottages or boardinghouses owned by once genteel Southern whites in The *Autumn Garden* and *Toys in the Attic*. Her settings, largely living rooms which act as battlegrounds for opposing socioeconomic views, metaphorically represent the nation during times of crisis and serve to raise questions of power and its abuse.

While Wilson, too, is concerned with power and its abuse, his point of view is necessarily a very different one. His role is that of the shaman/healer urging his characters to tell African American history in a vernacular fashion. He gives voice to those previously considered historyless in a construction of history which is also a quest for the black man's sense of identity in twenti-eth-century America. Wilson layers his *lieux de mémoire* in the blues, in ac-tual black historical figures (mentioned and characterized), and primarily in the Pittsburgh ghetto he calls home. While setting *Ma Rainey's Black Bottom* in a Chicago white-owned and controlled recording studio, Wilson discov-ered that the white man's turf pre-empted the free expression of African American behavior and his invasion of the space called forth misdirected violence. Wilson then decided to create a safe environment in the private en-clave of the Hill District where blacks could share their music, their business, and their life experiences through stories harkening back to the slavery and Reconstruction. Yet his cocoon fails to protect the black man from himself. King Hedley killed Floyd Barton because the singer, caught up in the Ameri-can desire for money and success, sacrificed the black boy Poochie in a bur-glary and refused to share his ill-gotten wealth with other black men.

Over the journey of the six dramas, Wilson explores a situation that Hellman could not have experienced in the same way. She certainly exam-ined the economic parity with men and independence denied to women in *The Little Foxes, Another Part of the Forest* and *Toys in the Attic.* Hers is primarily a drama dealing with individual empowerment and civic responsi-bility. Wilson, dealing with the history of the black man considered property to be bought and sold at will with its concomitant shattering of family struc-ture, had to expose the deep-seated insecurity and divisiveness within the black community itself before the full realization of expected civil rights could occur. Like Bynum, August Wilson is the "binding man" who coaxes and allows his characters to find their personal value in making music; shar-ing stories of slavery, reconstruction, chain gangs, prison; succeeding in sports; buying their own homes or farms; finding new jobs as truck drivers, entertainers or military officers; developing their own businesses. For those dispossessed of family since slavery began, the solution to self-determination lies in the solidarity of the African American community aware of its past and its current place in America. Both writers understand that historic aware-ness underlies a sense of identity as a unique person and as a citizen.

While separated by an entire generation as well as race and gender, Lillian Hellman and August Wilson, through their very differences, lead us to an understanding of a basic set of shared values expounded in such basic American documents as the Constitution and the Bill of Rights. Dedicated to the principles of self-determination, equal opportunity, a Puritan respect for hard work and a responsibility to one's community (whether nation or ethnic group), Hellman and Wilson use the theatre as an arena in which to explore their notion of the American Dream with its promise and its failings, as defined in the introduction by Toni Morrison. Attempting to achieve a better life free from the "poverty, prison, social ostracism and death" of the new world informs American immigrants, both free and slave. While Hellman constantly warns her public about invasions of freedom on the individual and national level, Wilson criticizes the enormous discrepancy between the promise of freedom and its failure in practice for African Americans. For Wilson, its accomplishment allows blacks to develop a new identity. In the difficult journey from property to person, the black man needs to recognize his past in order to build a better future, to discover a "new raiment of self."

As political activists, both Hellman and Wilson are moralists active in the artistic arena. Hellman utilizes her personal experience of Southern life and black folks, labor organizing to combat the dire poverty of the Depression, front-line reportage during World War II, and defense of Free Speech before the House Un-American Activities Committee. She champions women's rights in the work force and actively participates in the March on Washington to promote civil rights. While she was marching on the Capitol, August Wilson was learning about Black Power from Malcolm X, about poetic and polemical drama asserting the beauty of the black man and the leadership role of the artist from Amiri Baraka and about methods—translated by Karenga's *US* from rural Africa to urban America—to develop the African American community, celebrate its accomplishments, and share in a collective economy.

Both writers chose the theatre as a place to entertain and to teach. The theories of Jürgen Habermas, who believes in subjecting a "life world" to rational analysis and the possibility of communicative action through language, and David Ingram's conclusion that the dominance of money in capitalist democracies threatens the "justice of pluralities," apply to their work. These two expose different "life worlds" in American society to enable better understanding between the characters onstage and between performers and public.

They are both writers of moral purpose who rewrite history to fulfill their goals. Hellman uses the techniques of "you are there" reportage as she places her audience as spectators to fictionalized dramatizations or references to documented events. Wilson, on the other hand, without the benefit of a written "master narrative," creates an African American history conveyed through anecdotal "loud talking" and his blues ideology. *Lieux de mémoire* reside in geographic sites, actual events, music and even geography. While both employ living rooms, porches, and boarding houses as settings for their plays in metaphorical fashion, they resonate in different ways. Hellman contrasts the "haves" and "have nots" in specific eras of American history. She warns against the powerful attraction of money and wealth and with its ruthless exploitation of those on a lower economic level (including African Americans). She also exposes the danger of careless irresponsibility towards national issues of unemployment and threats to free speech. Writing prior to the Civil Rights movement, Hellman retains the white/black hierarchy in her dramas but imbues her African American nannies with great moral character. On the other hand, Wilson considers the black/white interface as a primarily economic one in which the white man is interested in the black only so long as the black man makes him money. Because of his perception of continued exploitation, Wilson, with the exception of *Ma Rainey's Black Bottom*, moves all his settings and cocoons his characters within the black community of Pittsburgh's Hill District to enable his characters to give voice to their history from slavery to the present in an environment segregated from the white hegemony. For both writers, personal empowerment is crucial to free and meaningful participation in American society.

Bibliography

Abrahams, Roger D. *Deep Down in the Jungle: Negro Narrative Folklore from the Streets of Philadelphia*. Chicago: Aldine Publishing, 1970.

Adams, Peter. *Conversations with Lillian Hellman*. Jackson: UP of Mississippi, 1986.

Baraka, Amiri (LeRoi Jones). *Dutchman and The Slave*. New York: Morrow Quill Paperbacks, 1964.

———— *Four Black Revolutionary Plays*. Indianapolis and New York: The Bobbs-Merrill Company, 1969.

———— *The Leroi Jones/Amiri Baraka Reader*. New York: Thunder's Mouth Press, 1991.

Barksdale, Richard and Keneth Kinnamon. *Black Writers of America*. New York: Macmillan, 1972.

Benjamin, Walter. *Illuminations*. Hannah Arendt, ed. Harry Zohn, trans. New York: Schocken Books, 1969.

Bills, Steven H. *Lillian Hellman, An Annotated Bibliography*. New York: Garland Publishing, Inc, 1979.

Elam, Harry J. *"Ma Rainey's Black Bottom*: Singing Wilson's Blues." *American Drama* (Spring 1996), 76–99.

Elkins, Marilyn, ed. *August Wilson: A Casebook*. New York: Garland Publishing, Inc., 1994.

d'Entrèves, Maurizio Passerin and Seyla Benhabib, eds. *Habermas and the Unfinished Project of Modernity: Critical Essays on the Philosophical Discourse of Modernity, Studies in Contemporary German Social Theory*. Cambridge: Polity Press, 1996.

Estrin, Mark W. *Lillian Hellman: Plays, Films, Memoirs*. Boston: G.K. Hall, 1980.

———— ed. *Critical Essays on Lillian Hellman*. Boston: G.K. Hall, 1989.

Fabre, Genevieve and Robert O'Meally, eds. *History and Memory in African-American Culture*. New York: Oxford UP, 1994.

Falk, Doris V. *Lillian Hellman*. New York: Frederick Ungar Publishing Co., 1978.

Feibleman, Peter. *Lilly: Reminiscences of Lillian Hellman*. New York: Avon Books, 1988.

Gates, Henry Louis, Jr. *The Signifying Monkey: A Theory of Afro-American Literary Criticism*. New York & Oxford: Oxford UP, 1988.

Giddens, Anthony. *Social Theory and Modern Sociology*. Stanford: Stanford UP, 1987.

Gilroy, Paul. *The Black Atlantic: Modernity and Double Consciousness*. Cambridge, MA: Harvard UP, 1993.

———— *Small Acts: Thoughts on the Politics of Black Cultures*. New York: Serpent's Tail, 1993.

Grant, Nathan L. "Men, Women, and Culture: A Conversation with August Wilson." *American Drama* (Spring 1996), 100–122.

Hellman, Lillian. *The Children's Hour*. Video recording. Culver City, CA: MGM/UA Home Video, 1990.

Hellman, Lillian. *The Collected Plays*. Boston & Toronto: Little, Brown & Co., 1972.

———— *Three: An Unfinished Woman, Pentimento, Scoundrel Time*. Boston & Toronto: Little, Brown & Co., 1979.

———— *Maybe*. Boston & Toronto: Little, Brown & Co., 1980.

———— *An Interview with Lillian Hellman*. Sound recording. Guilford, CT: Jeffrey Norton Publishers, 1969.

———— *The Little Foxes*. Video recording. Los Angeles: Embassy Home Entertainment, 1985.

———— *The North Star*. Video recording. Los Angeles: NTA Home Entertainment, 1984.

———— *Pentimento*. Boston & Toronto: Little, Brown & Co., 1973.

———— *Six Plays*. New York: Vintage Books, 1979.

———— *Toys in the Attic*. New York: Random House, 1960.

———— *Watch on the Rhine*. Video recording. Farmington Hills, MI: Key Video, 1984.

Hellman, Lillian/Hemingway, Ernest. *The Spanish Earth*. Video recording. Chicago: Facets Video, 1990.

hooks, bell. *A Postmodern Reader*. New York: State University of New York P, 1993.

Karenga, Maulana. *The African American Holiday of Kwanzaa*. Los Angeles: University of Sankore Press, 1988.

Karenga, Maulana. *Introduction to Black Studies*. Inglewood, CA: Kawaida Publications, 1982.

———— *Kwanzaa*. Inglewood, CA: Kawaida Publications, 1977.

Lederer, Katherine. *Lillian Hellman*. Boston: G.K. Hall & Co., 1979.

Malcolm X. *Malcolm X Speaks*. New York: Grove Press, 1965.

Mellen, Joan. *Hellman and Hammett*. New York: Harper Collins, 1996.

Moody, Richard. *Lillian Hellman: Playwright*. New York: The Bobbs-Merrill Company, Inc., 1972.

Morrison, Toni. *Playing in the Dark: Whiteness and the Literary Imagination*. New York: Vintage Books, 1992.

Nadel, Alan. *May All Your Fences Have Gates: Essays on the Drama of August Wilson*. Iowa City: U of Iowa P, 1994.

Nora, Pierre. *Les Lieux de Mémoire*. English: *Realms of Memory: Rethinking the French Past*. Lawrence D. Kritzman, ed. Arthur Goldhammer, trans. New York: Columbia UP, 1996. vol. 1.

Pereira, Kim. *August Wilson and the African-American Odyssey*. Urbana: U of Illinois P, 1995.

Powers, Kim. "An Interview with August Wilson." *Theater* (Fall/Winter, 1984), 50–55.

Riordan, Mary Marguerite. *Lillian Hellman, A Bibliography, 1926–1978*. Metuchen, NJ: Scarecrow Press, 1980.

Rollyson, Carl. *Lillian Hellman: Her Legend and Her Legacy*. New York: St. Martin's Press, 1988.

Savran, David. *In Their Own Words: Contemporary American Playwrights*. New York: TCG Inc., 1988.

Shannon, Sandra Garrett. *The Dramatic Vision of August Wilson*. Washington, DC: Howard UP, 1995.

Wilson, August. *Three Plays: Ma Rainey's Black Bottom, Fences, Joe Turner's Come and Gone*. Pittsburgh, PA: U of Pittsburgh P, 1991.

———— *The Piano Lesson*. New York: Penguin (Plume), 1990.

———— *Two Trains Running*. New York: Penguin (Plume), 1996.

———— *Seven Guitars*. New York: Penguin (Plume), 1992.

———— *Fences*. New York: Plume, 1986.

———— *Joe Turner's Come and Gone*. New York: Plume, 1988.

———— *Ma Rainey's Black Bottom*. New York: Plume, 1985.

———— *The Piano Lesson*. New York: Plume, 1990.

———— *Two Trains Running*. New York: Plume, 1992.

———— Interviews With Margaret Booker. Unpublished. Stanford: Stanford University, 1997.

———— *Jitney*. Unpublished manuscript. Crossroads Theatre Production Script, 1997.

———— "The Ground on Which I Stand." *American Theatre* (New York, 9/96), 72.

Wright, William. *Lillian Hellman: The Image, The Woman*. New York: Simon and Schuster, 1986.

Index

MODERN AMERICAN LITERATURE
New Approaches

Yoshinobu Hakutani, *General Editor*

The books in this series deal with many of the major writers known as American realists, modernists, and post-modernists from 1880 to the present. This category of writers will also include less known ethnic and minority writers, a majority of whom are African American, some are Native American, Mexican American, Japanese American, Chinese American, and others. The series might also include studies on well-known contemporary writers, such as James Dickey, Allen Ginsberg, Gary Snyder, John Barth, John Updike, and Joyce Carol Oates. In general, the series will reflect new critical approaches such as deconstructionism, new historicism, psychoanalytical criticism, gender criticism/feminism, and cultural criticism.

For additional information about this series or for the submission of manuscripts, please contact:

Peter Lang Publishing
P.O. Box 1246
Bel Air, MD 21014-1246

To order other books in this series, please contact our Customer Service Department at:

800-770-LANG (within the U.S.)
(212) 647-7706 (outside the U.S.)
(212) 647-7707 FAX

Or browse online by series at:

www.peterlangusa.com